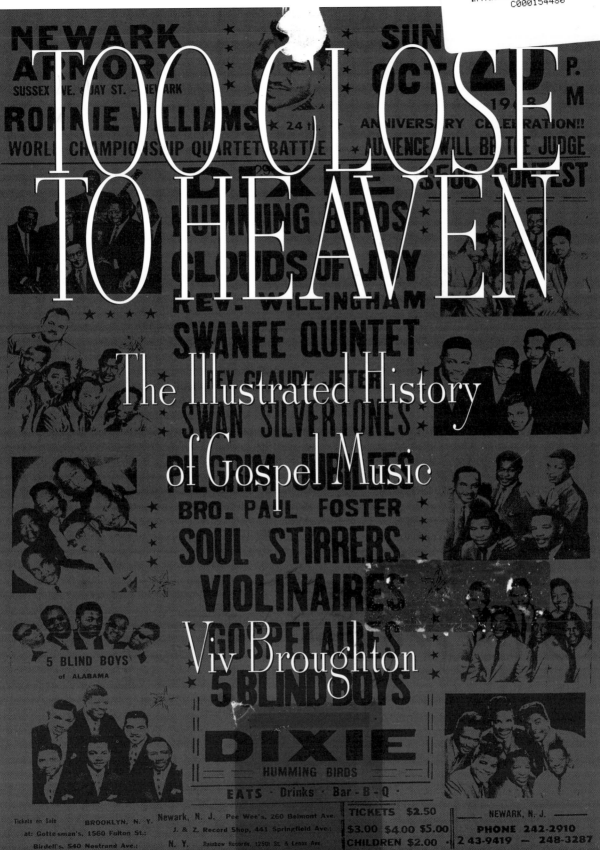

TOO CLOSE TO HEAVEN

The Illustrated History of Gospel Music

Viv Broughton

MIDNIGHT BOOKS, 32 SHIPTON STREET, LONDON E2 7RU, ENGLAND

Photo: 'Say Amen, Somebody'.

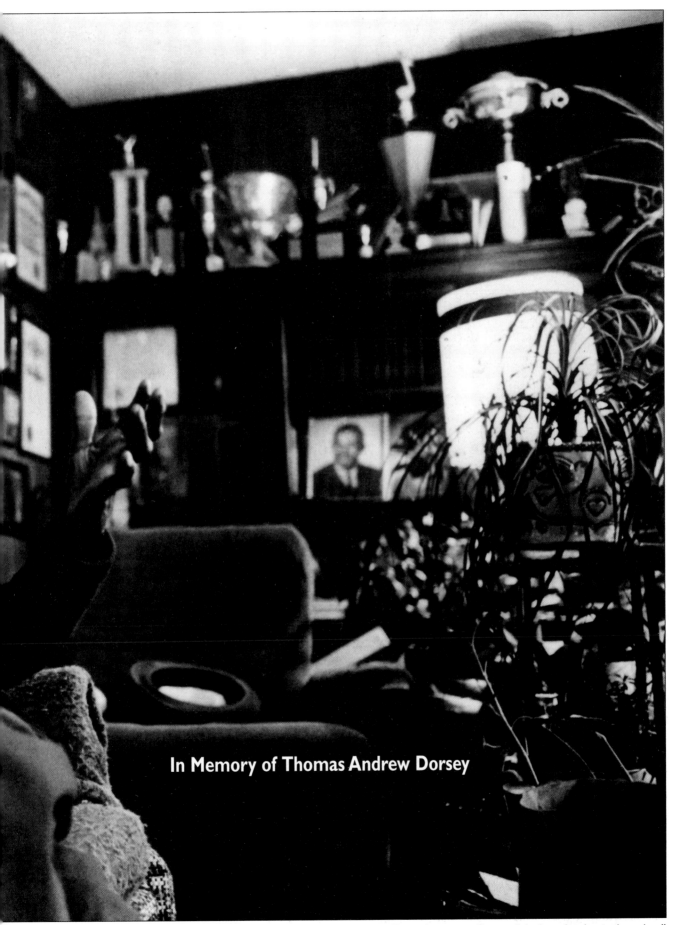

In Memory of Thomas Andrew Dorsey

"I was thrown out of some of the best churches in those days."
Thomas A. Dorsey, the Father of Gospel music, reminisces at home in Chicago.

Too Close To Heaven. The Illustrated History of Gospel Music.
Viv Broughton.

ISBN 1 900516 01 2 (hardback)
ISBN 1 900516 00 4 (paperback)

Typeset by Charlie O'Sullivan
Designed by Viv Broughton
Printed by Butler and Tanner Ltd, Frome.
Cover design by Dan Broughton
Cover photograph of Clara Ward by Terry Cryer
Back cover photographs of Kirk Franklin and Rev James Cleveland by Viv Broughton

British Library Cataloguing in Publication Data.
A catalogue record for this book is available from the British Library

For my sons Daniel, Matthew and Joe

My grateful thanks go to the following, who all gave invaluable help:

My Mother and Father, Nikki Collins, Charlie O'Sullivan, Del White, Paul Vernon, Nicola Ebenau, Gerard Rosenberg, Rev James Cleveland, Dorothy Love Coates, Bob Laughton, Kip Lornell, Leo St Clair, Alan Lewens, Roy Francis, Marcia Dixon, Sharron Wallace, Dan Broughton, Matthew Broughton, James Attlee, Dr Maya Angelou, J. W. Alexander, Gary Byrd, Lyn Abbott, Simon Albery, Tim Anderson, Chris Barber, Madeleine Bell, Ben Whitfield, Dr Margaret Douroux, Juliet Coley, Tony Cummings, Tony Heilbut, L.D. Frazier, Paul Oliver, Horst Lippman, Gentry McCreary, Earl Malone, Yvonne Twaits, Fred Mendelson, Anna Smallwood, Doug Seroff, Mattie Moss Clark, Judy Cheeks, Terry Cryer, Val Wilmer, Peter Grimsdale, Shirley Caesar, Jessy Dixon, Sasha Dalton, Teresa Hairston, Dr Bobby Jones, Marvin Winans, Ray Funk, Juliet Fletcher, Al Green, Charlie Gillet, Alexis Korner, Nick Fox, Opal Nations, Ed Smith, Geoff Heydon, Vy Higginson, Gary Hines, Petra Bernard, Dr James Collins, Ken Johnson, Dr Rose Jackson, Martin Jacox, P.J.O'Rourke, Clarence Fountain, Paul Jones, Ivan Chandler, Twinkie Clark, Rev Claude Jeter, Lawrence Cobb, Willy Leiser, Terry Jervis, Georgianne and Alvelyn Sanders, Al Matthews, Lee Magid, Tramaine Hawkins, Vicky Mack Lataillade, David Nathan, Anne Bennet-Nesby, Maureen and Michael Quinlan, Clive Richardson, Milton Biggham, Jesse Farley, Linda Reddin, Andrea Royer, Jeff Todd Titon, and all the good people at The Voice.

The following books were of immense help to me and they are emphatically recommended to anyone wishing to learn more about African-American Gospel music history:
We'll Understand It Better By and By. Bernice Johnson Reagon. *Smithsonian Institution Press.*
The Gospel Sound: Good News in Bad Times. Anthony Heilbut. *Anchor Press/Doubleday.*
How Sweet the Sound. Horace Boyer & Lloyd Yearwood. *Elliot and Clark.*
The Rise of Gospel Blues. The Music of Thomas Andrew Dorsey. Michael Harris. *Oxford University Press.*
Happy in the Service of the Lord. Kip Lornell. *University of Illinois Press.*

CONTENTS

Mother Willie Mae Ford Smith.

Photo: 'Say Amen, Somebody'

"There is no music like that music, no drama like the drama of the saints rejoicing, the sinners moaning, the tambourines racing, and all those voices coming together and crying holy unto the Lord. There is still, for me, no pathos quite like the pathos of those multi-coloured, worn, somehow triumphant and transfigured faces, speaking from the depths of a visible, tangible, continuing despair, of the goodness of the Lord.

I have never seen anything to equal the fire and excitement that sometimes, without warning, fills a church, causing the church (as Leadbelly and so many others have testified) to 'rock'. Nothing that has happened to me since, equals the power and the glory that I sometimes felt when, in the middle of a sermon, I knew that I was somehow, by some miracle, really carrying, as they said, 'the Word' - when the church and I were one. Their pain and their joy were mine, and mine were theirs. They surrendered their pain and joy to me, I surrendered mine to them - and their cries of 'Amen' and 'Hallelujah' and 'Yes Lord' and 'Praise His name!' and 'Preach it brother!' sustained and whipped on by solos until we all became equal, wringing wet, singing and dancing, in anguish and rejoicing, at the foot of the altar."

JAMES BALDWIN

Chicago's finest, the Barrett Sisters, c.1985.

INTRODUCTION

"I'm too close to heaven, can't turn around now..."

Alex Bradford's moving song of steadfast purpose, has been performed a thousand times in a thousand churches. Bessie Griffin offered up the definitive live recording of it at Mason's Temple in Memphis in 1953 and a rare performance of the song by the Five Blind Boys of Alabama graces the television series this book is based on. Implicit in the song is a declaration of intent understood by every gospel singer and every gospel congregation: we are on a journey of survival and the victory is near.

Gospel digs deeper than other music. Those who make it so - and those who have made it so in the past - form an uncompromising band of saints who have spent decades in contention with all manner of temporal demons. Where most performers sing out of their own artistic resources and for their own reward, any gospel singer worth half an amen will begin and end on an entirely different plane.

It's a disturbing kind of joy they dispense. It can hardly be tagged as entertainment, though it's often more entertaining than blues or soul or jazz or R&B or any of the other music with which it overlaps. Gospel is altogether more extreme in its depths and in its heights ... always at its best when at its most emotive and cathartic. This is, after all, a religious art-form concerned with life and death, invariably created under difficult circumstances. Few performers have had it quite so tough as gospel singers and it shows in the way they commit themselves within a song: diamond hard voices from way down on the human scale, rising up against all the odds to transcend the evil days and proclaim a special kind of victory.

A victory in the first instance over physical servitude. Bernice Johnson Reagon throws the early spirituals into sharp focus - *"Into our songs we worked the full range and intensity of our legacy in this land that made us slaves. Into our singing, we forged the sounds of people of a resolute spirit and fortitude in this land that debated our worth as human beings."* The Christian vision of deliverance from spiritual and social shackles has always held out the greatest hope to those with least to lose and the gospel song is essentially a song of deliverance. The real, breathtaking power of gospel singing cannot be understood as anything less than the ecstatic shout of a soul set free at last.

It's not necessarily a pleasurable experience for the uninitiated. Even a childhood steeped in the rites of the gospel church won't always prepare you for the upset created by a certain song or a certain singer at an uncertain moment. For an outsider coming upon the dramatic fervour of gospel unprepared, the effect can be utterly overwhelming. Disturbing even. *"There's something about the gospel blues,"* said Sister

9

Rosetta Tharpe to writer Tony Heilbut, *"that's so deep the world can't stand it."*

Which goes some way to explain, though not excuse, the neglect that gospel music has suffered from the world at large. Even though strains of the gospel sound are heard throughout the world of popular music, even though 'negro spirituals' (in multi-diluted form) are known by school children everywhere, even though virtually every significant African-American singer since the 1950s has graduated from gospel, very little is generally known about gospel music itself.

This book, and the television series it accompanies, is not the whole story by any means. The full glorious history of spiritual and gospel music is so vast and so complex and even now still so hidden, that I can only hope to introduce the major figures and events that shaped this most remarkable of Christian cultures. It isn't the definitive historical record any more than it is a musicological analysis of gospel; rather, it is offered as one doorway between the music and the world ... opening in on the band of saints who made (are still making) some of the most extraordinary vocal music the world has ever heard, and opening out so that their good news may be more widely heard.

However you experience gospel music, whether as believer or not, I hope you'll use this book to also dig a little deeper. Beneath the drama and excitement, maybe you'll discover the infinite wisdoms and jubilations that pulse through this music, quite apart from what is actually being articulated. There are echoes here that go way back to St Augustine in his Commentary on the Psalms:

> 'We acknowledge our inability to express in words what our heart is singing ...whenever people singing at the harvest, in the vineyards, or elsewhere in the ardour of their work are so gladdened by the words of their song that their joy becomes too great to express in words, they leave the syllables be and burst into exultation ...And who beseems this jubilation more than the utterable God? And when you cannot utter it, and yet must not withhold it, what remains for you to do but jubilate and let your heart exult wordlessly by breaking down all barriers in the immeasurable fullness of your joy...'

Say amen, somebody. ❖

Viv Broughton
London, July 1996

NOTHING BUT THE BLOOD

Slavery and the Birth of Spirituals

The Southern States of North America in the early 1870's was a place of extreme danger for all African-Americans. The Civil War was still a bitter and bloody memory for the recently defeated Confederates - their military strength crushed, their lucrative enjoyment of slave labour outlawed, their racial arrogance deeply undermined. General Robert E. Lee may have agreed surrender terms five years before, but the political attachments to white supremacy were not to be so easily given up. The *Atlanta News* was raging:

> '*All pride is to be crushed within us, We are to be the slave; the Negro is to be the master... We have submitted long enough to indignities, and it is time to meet brute force with brute force. Every Southern state should swarm with White Leagues, and we should stand ready to act... our hate must be unquenchable, our war interminable and merciless.*'

The Ku Klux Klan was just the largest of several secret societies offering the means and opportunity for revenge on the newly liberated black population. In a myriad of ways, the entire power structure of the old South was now emotionally ranged against the ex-slaves, with both legislature and judiciary conniving in the terror and abuse being meted out indiscriminately. The Klan was on the rampage in every county - robbing, lynching, raping, whipping and burning with impunity. With no defence available, neither physical nor legal, black citizens were forced to petition Congress for emergency measures:

'We would respectfully state that life, liberty and property are unprotected among the coloured race...Organised bands of desperate and lawless men, mainly composed of soldiers of the late Rebel armies, armed, disciplined and disguised, and bound by oath and secret obligations, have by force, terror and violence subverted all civil society among coloured people, thus utterly rendering insecure the safety of persons and property, overthrowing all those rights which are the primary basis and objects of the government...The legislature has adjourned; they refused to enact any laws to suppress Ku Klux disorder. We regard them now as being licensed to continue their dark and bloody deeds under the cover of the dark night...We appeal to you as law-abiding citizens to enact some laws that will protect us and that will enable us to exercise the rights of citizens.'

In May 1870 and again a year later, Congress responded by passing the Ku Klux Klan Acts in an attempt to control the secret societies. Thousands of members were indicted, resulting in 1250 convictions. Nevertheless, though it served to curb the worst excesses of the South, it did little to transform the all-consuming hatred harboured by defeated whites towards an emergent black population. For at least a century, the South was to remain a volatile and dangerous territory for all African-Americans.

At this time and in these circumstances, the very first concert performances of black sacred music took place. On 6th October 1871, eleven singers left the Tennessee town of Nashville, travelling by train on what was to be a historical and epic journey. They were students - six women and five men - from Fisk University, one of several chartered institutions established by the American Missionary Society *'to give the freedmen a high and Christian education.'* With them were the school treasurer, Mr George L. White, a *'skilled young Negro pianist'* Ella Shepherd, and a teacher (Miss Wells) from a missionary school in Athens, Alabama, to chaperone the women students. To set out on such a journey was an act of the very greatest faith. Though they had already performed to local audiences (even collecting a favourable notice or two in the press), the wider American public had heard nothing of black music except minstrel novelties, and the little group had virtually no money with them other than the fare to their first stop - Cincinatti, Ohio.

George White had come up with the idea of a concert tour out of desperation over funds for the Fisk College, which had been in continuous financial difficulties since it opened its doors in 1866. In fact, White had put his own money and property forward as security, in the hope that the Fisk Jubilee Singers as they were later known, would be able to raise sufficient from their performances to continue the tour and send any surplus back for the Fisk building programme.

There was a degree of reluctance among some of the singers as Maggie Porter Cole, the original soprano, explained:

"The boys and girls could remember how their parents had sung the songs when they huddled together by river banks and on hillsides to worship ... the children felt that those things were sacred. They were for God

and for their parents' talks with God ... not for white men's ears."

Another member of the original company said,

"It was our fear that the coloured people would be grieved to have us expose the ignorance and weakness incident to the days of our degradation. We did not realise how these were genuine jewels we brought from our bondage."

Nevertheless, the financial needs of the college took priority over their reservations and they travelled northward on the off-chance that the more enlightened of the white church ministers would support them, let them sing in the churches and take up collections. They had expected to be away for just a few months but, after a series of rapturously received performances at Henry Ward Beecher's church in Brooklyn, their fame spread and invitations came thick and fast. In Boston, one newspaper critic wrote that their songs were *"rendered with a power and pathos never surpassed'.*

The following year, they arrived back in Boston to take part in the huge World Peace Jubilee of 1872. It was expected to be something of a highlight, but in fact they would have been simply hidden away as part of the massive Festival chorus, had it not been for a remarkable incident. During the singing of the Battle Hymn of the Republic, it became clear that a fiasco was imminent - the orchestra had begun on too high a pitch and the opening verses were a *'painful failure'.* In dramatic manner, the Jubilee Singers stepped into the breech: *"Every word ... rang through the great Coliseum as if sounded out of a trumpet. The great audience was carried away with a whirlwind of delight... Men threw their hats in the air and the Coliseum rang with cheers and shouts of 'The Jubilees! The Jubilees forever!'"*

The reputation of the Fisk Jubilee Singers was now firmly established, and on an international stage too. They began to travel abroad, singing to commoners and royalty in Europe. They visited Britain five times and were feted by English society. Queen Victoria, who is reported to have wept with joy when she heard them sing, commissioned their portrait, which now hangs in the entrance hall of Fisk University.

It is said that all this fulfilled a remarkable prophecy. John Wesley Work, one of the first music instructors at Fisk, recounted in 1915, the following story:

"A master of Tennessee plantation had sold a mother from her babe, and the day for the separation was fast approaching when the mother was to be taken 'down South'. Now, the condition of the slave in Tennessee was better than in any other state, with the possible exception of Virginia. To be sold 'South' was, to the slave, to make the journey from which no traveller ever returned. So it was not strange that the mother would sooner take her life and that of her babe, than to go down into Mississippi, which, to her, was going to her grave. Bent upon throwing herself and her child over the steep banks of the Cumberland River, she was stumbling along the dusty road, her infant clasped close to her breast, muttering in frenzy her dire determination, 'Before I'd be a slave, I'd be buried in my grave!' An old 'mammy', seeing the terrible expression on her face, and hearing these words, read her intentions. In love she laid her dear old hand upon the shoulder of the distressed mother and said, 'Don't you do it honey, wait, let de chariot of de Lord swing low, and let me take one of de Lord's scrolls an' read it to you.' Then, making a

Photo: Author's collection.
Poster courtesy of Fisk University.

GUILDHALL, PLYMOUTH,
Wednesday Evening, August 18th.

THE

JUBILEE SINGERS,

Ex-Slave Students from Fisk University, U.S.A.,

WILL GIVE A

Concert of Slave Songs,

IN THE

GUILDHALL, PLYMOUTH,

ON

WEDNESDAY EVENING, AUGUST 18th, 1875.

Doors open at ½-past 7. Concert begins at 8.

Seats, Reserved and Numbered, 3s. ; Unreserved Seats, 2s. ; Admission, 1s.

Tickets may be secured and Plan of the Hall seen at Moon & Sons' Pianoforte Saloon,
6 & 7, George Street.

THE JUBILEE SINGERS.

SECOND VISIT TO GREAT BRITAIN.

THIS band of ex-slave students from Fisk University, U.S.A., who two years ago made so many friends in Great Britain by their rendering of the weird slave melodies, have returned for a second tour. Additional funds are imperatively needed to complete the furnishing of Jubilee Hall, and to more fully equip the University in other respects for its work. By the violent emancipation of the war, the freed-men of America were left, empty-handed and ignorant, in the midst of their former masters, who were nettled by their enfranchisement and opposed, for the most part, to their education and social elevation. They need Christian sympathy from every quarter, and they need it *now*, before the impulse of the abrupt social changes of the war shall spend its force.

The Singers gratefully remember the cordial welcome they received on their first visit. They hope to be able, now, to meet at least some of the applications for concerts that it was im-possible for them to fill before. While five of the old Singers have felt obliged, for varying personal reasons, to retire, these vacancies have been happily filled, and the Company has suffered no loss of strength or distinctive character. They expect to give better concerts than ever before ; they hope to make them well worth all they shall cost those who attend them. And their ardent desire is that these little sums, so small singly as to be scarcely felt by those who pay them, may be so large in the aggregate as to make Fisk University not only a great power in the education and elevation of their own people in America, but, through their missionary labours, in the final evangelisation of Africa and the islands of the sea.

The original Fisk Jubilee Singers (Ella Shepherd seated at harmonium).
Inset: Poster for one of their concerts in England.

motion as reaching for something and unrolling it, she read, 'God's got a great work for dis baby to do; she's goin' to stand befo' kings and queens. Don't you do it, honey.' The mother was so impressed with the words of the old 'mammy' she gave up her fell design and allowed herself to be taken off down into Mississippi, leaving her baby behind."

The baby girl was Ella Shepherd, who later entered Fisk College and fulfilled the prophecy by becoming the original pianist of the Fisk Singers. The story also had a poignant post-script because, after the long tour was over, Ella set out southwards to try and find her mother. An almost hopeless task, but eventually she succeeded and brought her back to live in peace and comfort through her old age. Mrs Sarah Hannah Shepherd died peacefully in her sleep in the summer of 1912.

The epic tour of the Fisk Singers lasted an amazing seven years and raised the huge sum of $150,000, which was used to build a magnificent new Jubilee Hall at Fisk University, on the site of a former Union Army barracks. It was affectionately known as 'Frozen Music'.

For all their great international success though, the Fisk Jubilee Singers were something of an anomaly, eccentric to the norm of black music at the time. The audiences they sang to were overwhelmingly white, and the spirituals they sang were tailored accordingly. The Fisks were the first, but certainly not the last, African-American artists who dressed up the image and dressed down the music in order to crossover to the white market. As they themselves were quick to reassure the genteel church-goers who flocked to hear them, they had *'purged the songs of all ungainly africanism'*.

Even so, leading abolitionist and patron of the Fisks, Henry Ward Beecher, was warning friends in England that *'You will hear from them the wild slave songs, some of which seem like the inarticulate wails of breaking hearts made dumb by slavery'*. No doubt Victorian Britain appreciated the melodrama, but listening to the scratchy recordings that remain of the (later) Fisk Jubilee Singers, it is clear that, shrewd and skillful as they may have been in parting white audiences from their cash, the 'negro spirituals' themselves had already been anglicised out of all recognition. For at least twenty years, the Fisk Singers' success inspired a host of imitators - jubilee singing groups abounded, catering to the fashionable interest outside of the South in post-minstrelsy entertainment. Some even featured in travelling freak-shows and circuses.

Musical standards inevitably declined: *"The rule in the organisation of jubilee companies has been about two real singers with six or seven very, very rotten ones. The rotten singers, along with the 'whiskey heads' must be put on the incline plane of popular disapproval and sent down to oblivion,"* was one jubilee group director's disgusted opinion. Writing in 1901, a black theatre critic concluded that, during the 1890s ...

"...there was a wholesale letting down of the racial standard.... Even the whites were becoming inoculated, but remember, the songs did not refer to them. They gave the shekels to hear us sing away our honour and we sang."

Unfortunately, the popularised conception endures even to this day. Ask most white people what they think a 'negro spiritual' sounds like and they will attempt to describe something much like the expurgated songs of the Fisk Singers. There can be no doubting the courage, faith and endurance of the pioneer singers from the freedmen's colleges, but the real spirituals were a different music entirely.

The true roots of gospel music and spirituals can be traced to the extraordinary collision of cultures that took place at the beginning of the 18th century, as bonded African slave met the first flood of English church hymns on American soil. From as early as 1619, when the very first abducted African set foot in the (then) English colonies at Jamestown, Virginia, the Christian church was anxious for the souls of the new arrivals in their midst. It will be to its eternal shame that the European church effectively legitimised the trans-atlantic slave trade (one popular heresy of the time being that slaves were 'non-human' and therefore beyond salvation) but in comparison to the masters' brutality and enforcement, the influence of the church may be considered relatively benign.

Not until the beginning of the 18th century did the conversion of slaves proceed in earnest. The Society for the Propagation of the Gospel was established in London to supply and maintain missions in the Americas. At first there was great opposition, not just from slaves themselves who were suspicious of the white man's religion, but also from the masters, uneasy about any gatherings of slaves which might serve as a cloak for organised revolt. Laws were passed to control the work of missionaries, like this one passed in North Carolina in 1715:

> 'That if any master or owner of Negroes or slaves, or any other person or persons whatsoever in the government, shall permit or suffer any Negro or Negroes to build on their, or either of their lands, or any part thereof, any house under pretense of a meeting-house upon account of worship, or upon any pretense whatsoever, and shall not suppress and hinder them, he, she, or they so offending, shall, for every default, forfeit and pay fifty pounds, one-half toward defraying the contingent charges of the government, the other to him or them that shall sue for the same.'

In Maryland, a law was enacted in 1723 'to suppress tumultuous meetings of slaves on Sabbath and other holy days' and in Georgia, the constables were commanded to disperse any assembly or meeting of slaves 'which may disturb the peace or endanger the safety of His Majesty's subjects; and every slave which may be found at such a meeting may ... immediately be corrected, without trial, by receiving on the bare back twenty-five stripes, with a whip, switch or cowskin'.

Despite the laws and despite the violence, tribesmen and women from the Fon, the Yoruba, the Ibo, the Fanti, the Ashanti, the Mandingo and the Jolof, sustained themselves in their terrible exile with the only things, apart from life itself, which hadn't already been taken from them: the cultures and religions of their people. Precious West African traditions of chant, ritual, polyrhythm and dance are known to have survived attempts by the first masters to wipe them out. Some even survived into the twentieth century, like the 'ring shout' - a shuffling circular dance ritual that later became a feature of black Christian worship and fore-ran the 'holy dance' of today's gospel churches. The polytheistic heritage of Mother Africa was not to be so easily displaced by the alien God of Europe and the old faiths and customs remained strong for almost a century. Though there are records of slave baptism into the Christian church going back as far as 1641, the progress of religious instruction was slow.

When the Bishop of London inquired in 1724, 'Are there any Infidels, bond or free, within your Parish; and what means are used for their conversion?', he met with a disappointing response:

'Our Negroe Slaves imported daily, are altogether ignorant of God and Religion, and in truth have so little Docility in them that they scarce ever become capable of Instruction; but ... I have examined and improved Several Negroes, Natives of Virginia ...' (From James City Parish).

However, tribal memories were gradually suppressed, giving way to the harsh new realities of six days hard labour and rest on the Sabbath. Even the gross hypocrisy of Christian slave owners didn't usually extend to the violation of the fourth commandment and, using all their acquired skills of survival, slaves reluctantly embraced the only forms of worship and ritual permitted to them. One early catechism demonstrates the attempt to use religious instruction as a method of social control:

"What did God Make you for?"
"To make a crop."
"What is the meaning of 'Thou shalt not commit adultery?'"
"To serve our heavenly Father, and our earthly master, obey our overseer, and not steal anything."

It didn't fool everyone and the objective was often subverted. As one ex-slave put it:

"When I starts preaching I couldn't read or write and had to preach what Master told me, and he say tell them niggers iffen they obeys the Master they goes to Heaven; but I knowed there's something better for them, but daren't tell 'cept on the sly. That I done lots. I tells 'em iffen they keeps praying, the Lord will set 'em free."

All church music up to this point was confined to the singing of psalms in a 'grave and serious' manner - that is, at a snail's pace and devoid of instrumentation. Though preferable in entertainment value to the interminable pulpit preachers, it was hardly a substitute for the exuberances of Africa. Even white churchgoers were becoming dissatisfied with the dreary psalms as a suitable means of praising God.

The new religious movement that swept through the colonies in the 1730s was known as the 'Great Awakening' and chief among its features was the use of new hymns in place of scriptural psalms. It may not seem such a tremendous development to us today, but it was profoundly significant to the patterns of worship - and therefore music - at the time. Both black and white were caught up in great waves of fervour over the new hymnody. Slaves especially, seized upon the stirring, lively tunes of a certain Non-conformist English minister - Dr Isaac Watts.

Dr Watts was an unlikely and unwitting catalyst for African-American music - his name isn't normally linked to the illustrious voices of gospel and soul. There's no doubt at all though, that he must be considered the single most important composer in the early history of spiritual song in America. Born in Southampton on 17th July 1674, Isaac Watts spurned the offer of a university education and ordination in the Church of England, entering a Non-conformist academy in the then London hamlet of Stoke Newington in 1690. He joined the independent congregation at the Girdlers' Hall which still stands near Moorgate in the City, returning briefly to Southampton, where he wrote the bulk of his most influential work *Hymns and Spiritual Songs*, first published in 1707. He died in 1748 and is buried in the Puritan resting-place at Bunhill Fields in the old City of London. His legacy is a mass of more than four hundred

Five generations of a slave family in South Carolina.

hymns, psalms and spirituals that can still be heard today throughout the diaspora churches.

Quite why the hymns of a Non-conformist Englishman should have so captured the imagination of slaves in America, is something of a mystery, but capture it they did. Many letters from colonial missionaries testify to their immense popularity. A Rev Mr Wright reports to England soon after the publication of *Hymns and Spiritual Songs* (in Boston 1739):

> 'My landlord tells me, when he waited on the colonel at his country seat two or three days, they heard the Slaves at worship in their lodge, singing Psalms and Hymns in the evening and again in the morning, long before break of day. They are excellent singers, and long to get some of Dr Watts' Psalms and Hymns, which I encouraged them to hope for.'

The conventional wisdom has it that Watts' hymns caught on so forcefully with slave congregations because they offered lively tunes and engaging poetry and because the English practice of 'lining' these hymns - whereby a minister or some other appointed person would chant out each line for the congregation to repeat - also accorded with the African tradition of call-and-response. I would suggest that, in addition to this, these hymns brought hope and strength to an oppressed people. Dr Watts, and other great 18th century hymnwriters, were able to capture so completely the Christian vision of blessedness for the poor, rest for the weary and deliverance for the captive, that they altogether transcended the cultural divide. The so-called 'Era of Watts' had begun and there was no stopping it.

Other English hymnwriters followed in Watts' footsteps: John Wesley, who had founded the Methodist Church with his brother Charles, published *A Collection of Psalms and Hymns* - half of them by Isaac Watts. John Newton, born in London in 1732, was to write one of the most famous and enduring spirituals - *Amazing Grace* - often credited wrongly to Watts. There is an especial irony in this, since Newton had himself spent fifteen months 'in abject degradation under a slave-dealer in Africa' before escaping and commanding his own slave ship for six years. All prior to a dramatic Christian conversion and the authorship of his most universal spiritual song - but it's certainly curious to think, as you listen to Aretha Franklin or Tramaine Hawkins singing *Amazing Grace*, that this great hymn of solace for a race in captivity was penned by a former slave ship captain.

By the time of the American Revolution in 1775, African-Americans comprised nearly a quarter of colonial society, though performing a rather greater proportion of the physical labour that sustained it. It was still, for the most part, a cruelly debilitating existence - but there were signs that the beginning of the end of slavery was near. The first of many anti-slavery societies was set up by the Quakers in Philadelphia. In England, the end of slavery had already been signalled three years before and the British Army was quick to exploit the slight moral advantage, undermining the American independence movement from within, by offering freedom to any slaves who enlisted. Hundreds responded, but many more remained loyal and joined the colonists' struggle for independence. More than five thousand slaves fought the seven year war, not for their own freedom and self-government, but for that of their masters.

Many slaves though, sensed that momentous changes were in the air - changes that would, or could,

Top: A first edition of Isaac Watts' 1707 Hymnal.
Below: Dr Watts.

Top: Bishop Richard Allen, founder of the African Methodist
Episcopal Church. Below: Richard Allen's original hymnal.

improve their wretched lot. As has so often happened in history, the Christian church - almost despite itself - became the focus of political evolution. The Sabbath was still the only day of rest for slaves and the churches were by now drawing large slave congregations. The Methodists especially, had recruited a large black membership, but the Baptists too were rapidly overtaking the main Church of England in mission activities. Notwithstanding the complicity of ministers and clergy in the system of slavery, the various biblical messages of hope and liberation could not forever be obscured, eventually transcending the misdeeds and shortcomings of the missionaries. The messenger was about to be overtaken by the message and the African-American church was soon to be born.

The first African in America to be granted a licence to preach was one George Leile, a slave belonging to a Baptist deacon in Kiokee, Georgia. Around 1780 he helped set up the African Baptist Church in Savannah - the first such congregation in America. Thereafter, and throughout African-American history, the Baptist church formed a vanguard of leadership - Rev Martin Luther King Jr and Rev Jesse Jackson being just two of its many great sons.

Perhaps the most significant figure of the time though, both in terms of black independence and black music, was Richard Allen. Born a slave in Philadelphia in 1760, he took advantage of the liberalising of the law in the North and purchased his freedom at the age of seventeen. He became an itinerant Methodist preacher, eventually assigned to the Old St George's Methodist Episcopal Church in Philadelphia - at that time the capital city of the new United States.

He began to draw large congregations - both black and white - but as the numbers of black worshippers increased, so did the hostility of white parishioners, who wanted them 'removed from their original seats and placed around the wall'. During one particular service in 1787, an act of racism occurred which was to trigger the whole independent black church movement and, as we shall see, hasten the development of spiritual music. A group of black church members, including associate minister Absalom Jones and Allen himself, were set upon by white deacons who pulled them from their knees while praying. Such an extreme outrage by his fellow 'brothers in the Lord' decided Richard Allen for separatism: '...we all went out of the church in a body, and they were no more plagued with us in the church.'

Richard Allen and Absalom Jones jointly set up the Free African Society. But within seven years, the two pioneer clergymen had diverged: Jones to found the African Episcopal Church, which quickly affiliated to the main white Episcopal denomination; Allen to establish the ultimately more influential African Methodist Episcopal Church entirely separate from the white Methodist Church. He did not however renounce Methodism itself: 'I was confident that no religious sect or denomination would suit the capacity of the coloured people so well as the Methodists, for the plain simple gospel suits best for any people, for the unlearned can understand and the learned are sure to understand.'

Allen's church - Mother Bethel as it was called - was inaugurated in 1794, electing him the first black bishop of America twenty two years later, to oversee the many branches and members. The AME today is one of the largest of the African-American denominations.

The significance of Richard Allen for this history however, lies with his celebrated hymnal, published in

1801 and titled *A Collection of Spiritual Songs and Hymns Selected From Various Authors by Richard Allen, African Minister.* It is the clearest evidence we have today of the songs that enjoyed greatest popularity among black congregations at the start of the 19th century, confirming the ascendancy of Dr Watts' compositions together with Wesleyan and Baptist hymns and several written by Allen himself. The most popular hymn of all with African-Americans throughout this period, was the Watts' composition *When I Can Read My Title Clear* (No. 26 in Allen's collection). This collection also provides us with one of the most important sources of black church music as it metamorphosed into 'negro spirituals'.

The African Methodists came under fierce verbal attack from other Methodists, not least for their 'noisy' styles of worship. One prominent white critic wrote caustically:

> 'We have too, a growing evil in the practice of singing in our places of worship, merry airs, adapted from old songs, to hymns of our composing: often miserable as poetry and senseless as matter ... Most frequently composed and first sung by the illiterate blacks of the Society.'

What was happening of course was that an indigenous folk music of praise, worship and lament was in the process of being born. It could not be truly identified any more as being strictly in the English hymn tradition - hence the consternation of the white church critics. Nor could it be acknowledged as wholly African, though it drew upon the many conventions and styles of mother Africa. These new hymns were still in large part those of Dr Watts, adapted for the practical use of a community with a healthy disrespect for purism, who added their own choruses, verses, stanzas or refrains and, increasingly, joined them to the African pentatonic (5-note) scale, sometimes adding the 'flatted seventh' - that note of melancholy which also characterises the secular blues.

Eventually, the original tune was almost unrecognisable and, with the lyrics now a folk interpretation with a rough sense of the original, it can be seen that entirely new songs emerged. The connections can still be easily spotted though. Take the ancient spiritual rendered most perfectly by the Harmonizing Four of Richmond, Virginia (in the following century) as:

> My Lord, what a morning,
> My Lord, what a morning,
> My Lord, what a morning,
> When the stars begin to fall.
>
> You will hear the trumpet sound
> To wake the nations underground,
> Looking to my God's right hand,
> When the stars begin to fall.

This can be directly traced to verses of Hymn No. 10 in Allen's original Hymnal:

> Behold the awful trumpet sounds,
> The sleeping dead to raise,

And calls the nations underground:
O how the saints will praise!

The falling stars their orbits leave,
The sun in darkness hide:
The elements asunder cleave,
The moon turn'd into blood!

Behold the universal world
In consternation stand,
The wicked unto Hell are turn'd
The Saints at God's right hand.

John Wesley Work, one of the earliest black historians, confirms the process of adaptation:

"In truth, the uninitiated would not recognise the best known hymn sung thus, unless he could catch a familiar word every now and then. An example of variation may be found in such songs as 'I've Been Redeemed'. The chorus is Negro, but the stanzas of 'There Is A Fountain Filled With Blood' are used."

There are dozens of similar songs traceable directly to the old hymns of Dr Watts and his contemporaries, providing the route whereby many of the new spirituals emerged. In the cities at least, an indigenous black music was being forged for the first time in the New World, reflecting all the pre-occupations of slavery and deliverance.

Further South in the rural heartlands of America, a similar process was taking place around the phenomenon of the 'camp meetings', which captured the imagination of frontier communities during a massive revival movement spanning fifty years from around 1780. The revival was known as the 'Second Awakening' and it fired the religious zeal of the common people of all the Protestant denominations, both black and white. Led by the evangelical pioneers of Methodism, seized upon by the Baptists and other Non-conformist sects, the Second Awakening placed religious experience before theological doctrine and introduced pentecostal fire to the masses. Extended and extempore prayers, dramatic conversions, glossolalia (the gift of tongues), shouting in the Spirit, ecstatic baptism, mass baptism and spiritual healing all began to be common, corresponding to a new urgency and populism in church music. The Anglican attachment to dreary psalms was being superseded by soul-stirring hymns and songs, more closely expressing the simple faith and immediate concerns of the people. In Britain, Methodism was sowing the seeds of socialist reform; in America, it produced a different kind of popular activism.

In July 1800, thousands of people flocked to a historic first camp meeting organised by a Presbyterian minister, Reverend James McGready, but involving a number of different churches. It was set up in the middle of a forest in Logan County, Kentucky ... a week-long mass rally of worshippers in tents of every shape and size. At night, so many fires were lit around the camp that it appeared almost as if the entire forest was aflame. The experiment was instantly a huge success and the phenomenon spread throughout Kentucky and then in all directions across the country.

Below: Abolitionist and former slave Frederick Douglass.

Top: Harriet Tubman, far left, with slaves she helped escape.
Below: Harriet Tubman, known as 'Black Moses'.

These vast gatherings in the open air - anything up to twenty thousand people at a time - were quite without precedent and defy rational explanation. The main tent was usually a circus style big-top (known as the tabernacle) where fiery itinerant evangelists held sway, preaching for up to four hours at a stretch. Interspersed between the sermons were marathon sessions of congregational singing - hour upon hour of evangelistic hymns and choruses. Once again, the name of Dr Watts appears, his compositions enjoying enormous popularity with camp audiences.

Perhaps they sound like exhausting occasions to us today, but there was a distinct holiday atmosphere in the camp meetings, especially for slaves attuned to the endless routine of back-breaking work in rice and cotton plantations. The camp offered festive relief, a chance to sing and shout, a chance to do more than fetch and carry. Hardly surprising then that slaves flocked to the camps, sometimes outnumbering the whites and usually dominating the singing. Though camp meetings were almost always inter-racial, strict segregation prevailed in the seating or standing arrangements and this served to set up intense rivalries in singing power. One visitor to a camp in Georgia remembered the spontaneous 'choirs' that formed:

> "Most likely the sound proceeded from the black portion of the assembly, as their number was three times that of the whites, and their voices are naturally beautiful and pure."

At another camp meeting in Pennsylvania, black singers among the 7000 strong crowd prompted an observer to comment, 'Their shouts and singing were so very boisterous that the singing of the white congregation was often completely drowned in the echoes and reverberations of the coloured people's tumultuous strains!' Nor was it at all unusual for the black camp members to carry on singing long after their white counterparts had retired to bed. 'At about half-past five the next morn ... the hymns of the Negroes were still to be heard on all sides.'

Interestingly, there is also much evidence that some of the rituals of Africa re-emerged at the camp meetings. Surreptitiously of course and suitably Christianised, but quite distinctly African in origin. Like the ring-shouts - circles of chanting singers, half-dancing, half-marching, stamping out the tempo on each word of a drawn-out chorus, sometimes complementing the rhythm with hand claps or thigh slaps. The final morning of camp meetings often featured the 'weird spectacle' of an enormous ring-shout completely encircling the whole camp. All the slave worshippers, having sung and worshipped throughout the previous night, now shuffled, chanted, danced and shouted in a spectacular sunrise farewell march.

The camp meetings produced spirituals in much the same way that the new African churches in the cities produced spirituals - as an uneven synthesis of African chant and English hymn. In fact, some of the choruses which formed the basis of several spirituals and which were most popular with camp audiences (white as well as black), first appear in that hymnal of Richard Allen and the African Methodists. Illiteracy was widespread of course and in any case, copies of Allen's hymnal itself were scarce (copies of any hymnal were scarce), so that the hymns were passed from person to person by memory.

Inevitably, some parts of hymns were lost or became mixed up with other hymns, some were re-expressed in colloquialisms, some were lost completely. The most memorable therefore, and the most apposite versions, formed the raw materials of most 19th century African-American religious songs.

Other spirituals were born directly out of the camp experience itself, like the one that appears in John Wesley Work's collection:

Going to moan and never tire
Moan and never tire
Moan and never tire
There's a great camp meeting in the promised land

This spiritual, composed in secret by a company of slaves who had been forbidden to sing, is also interesting because it records the 'moan', which paradoxically isn't a moan at all but a joyful vocal expression of deep spiritual significance. John Wesley Work again:

"In the big meetings there was a certain set of church members set aside to lead in the moaning, a low plaintive fragment of melody, sometimes a hum and sometimes accompanied by words of striking character. This is done to help the preacher as he pours out his sermon, which is generally a vivid description of hell and destruction awaiting the sinner."

Gradually, a recognisable body of songs emerged to become the first modern folk music of America - religious in character and pre-dating blues, jazz and gospel itself. The plantation hymns of the slave nation now acquired a momentum of their own, and new spirituals began to be added that owed less to England and Africa and more to the realities of survival in the New World. Now that the spiritual had established its own identity as a true folk music, entirely original songs started to appear that cannot be traced to any particular hymn or chant.

These expressed the faith of the slaves themselves. They mourned the tragedies of a slave existence, they celebrated hope in hopeless circumstances and they raised the prospect of eventual deliverance. The new spirituals were born out of the slave's own perception of divinity within bondage. Often they were tales of particular incidents, events and experiences - unique to one person but common to many.

Sarah Hannah Shepherd's story of prophetic deliverance on the banks of the Cumberland River, saving her and her daughter from suicide, is the reputed source of not one, but two of the most famous spirituals of all - *Before I'd Be A Slave, I'd Be Buried In My Grave* and the quintessential *Swing Low, Sweet Chariot*. The two songs burst *'from the same soul of anguish, from the same heart at the same time and under the same condition.'* The story runs that, after her reunion with daughter Ella following the Fisk Singers tour, Mother Shepherd lived in love and comfort until the *'sweet chariot swung low'* in 1912. On her deathbed *'... she had been unconscious for some hours, but when she heard the strains of this, her heart-born song which was being sung at her bedside, she awoke and made a supreme effort to join in the melody.'*

Other spontaneous spirituals were born *'out of hearts in a state of almost religious frenzy.'* That is, they were composed on the spot in church services:

"Go out among the rural churches today and attend the Big Meetings, and there will spring up before your very eyes the first fresh shouts of songs which are soon to flourish and fructify. During slavery in

some localities it was a custom to require each new convert, before allowing him to 'join the church' to sing a new song..."

Some spirituals like *Steal Away To Jesus* and *Go Down Moses, Let My People Go* were of both sacred and subversive intent, similes for either temporary or permanent escape:

"On a plantation down on the Red River, in the early part of the nineteenth century, a master of a large number of slaves was accustomed to allow them to go across the river, at stated times, that they might worship with the Indians, who had a mission there. They always enjoyed themselves, and talked much of the good times on the other side. But one day the master learned that the missionary to the Indians was a northern man; and, believing that he might put ideas of freedom in the heads of his slaves prohibited his slaves from worshipping any more across the river. Doubtless the master thought the matter was settled then and there, but not so; the slaves could not forget the good times across the river; and what they could not do in the open they determined to do in secret. They decided to 'Steal away to Jesus', as one slave expressed it. 'Steal away to Jesus' whispered at first, later chanted softly, was notice that that night there were to be services across the river. The first-born thought, 'Steal away to Jesus', was expressed all day, in the fields of cotton and of corn, and in fragments of tuneful melody the slaves were all informed of what would occur that night. At night when the master, overseer, and hounds had retired to sweet sleep, the slaves would steal away from their cabins and quietly creep through the cotton, corn and tall grasses, softly humming their greetings to one another. On toward the river they crept, and the night breezes wafted their melody to the ears of the missionary, who thereby knew that his black congregation was coming."

By the end of the 'Second Awakening' in 1830, the shout of freedom was following inexorably on from the cry for spiritual deliverance. Denmark Vesey had already led a massive revolt in South Carolina involving as many as nine thousand slaves. The first black newspaper *Freedom's Journal* was published in New York, followed in 1831 by William Lloyd Garrison's journal of militant anti-slavery *The Liberator*. The same year Nat Turner led his famous slave revolt in Virginia, prompting the organisation of the American Anti-Slavery Society.

Two decades of intense unrest over slavery consumed the entire country, bitterly dividing it between the abolitionist Northern States and the intransigent plantation barons of the South. Increasingly, enslaved African-Americans were breaking their own chains in order to stand and fight or to escape northward along the 'Underground Railroad' established by ex-slaves like Harriet Tubman and Frederick Douglass.

Religious imagery in song now took on a covert political significance, serving to communicate coded messages within slave conspiracies. The infinitely courageous Harriet Tubman, who made innumerable trips into the South to 'conduct' other flights to freedom, was known affectionately as 'Black Moses' and used the following spiritual to alert slaves to her arrival:

Dark and thorny is de pathway
Where de pilgrim makes his ways
But beyond dis vale of sorrow
Lie de fields of endless days.

Frederick Douglass, the great abolitionist, also used spirituals to sustain the hope of escape from slavery and later wrote:

> 'We were, at times, remarkably buoyant, singing hymns and making joyous exclamations, almost as triumphant in their tone as if we had reached a land of freedom and safety. A keen observer might have detected in our repeated singing of 'O Canaan, sweet Canaan, I am bound for the land of Canaan' something more than a hope of reaching heaven. We meant to reach the north - and the north was our Canaan.'

Although some 12 million Africans were transported during slavery, the official Census of 1860 claimed that at this time there were just 4,880,009 black people in the United States, of whom exactly ten per cent were free. A year later, Abraham Lincoln was inaugurated as the sixteenth President, and the remaining ninety per cent looked to him for their long-awaited liberation. On the day of his election, slaves in Georgetown, South Carolina were whipped for singing this spiritual:

> We'll fight for liberty
> We'll fight for liberty
> We'll fight for liberty
> Till the Lord shall call us home;
> We'll soon be free,
> Till the Lord shall call us home.

The Southern States were outraged at Lincoln's election, refused to accept his Presidency and promptly seceded to form the Confederate States of America under Jefferson Davis. Within months, the country was plunged into the horrendous Civil War that split the nation wide apart, taking the lives of 430 soldiers for every single day during the whole of the four year holocaust. For forty years, Northern whites had argued with Southern Whites over many conflicting ambitions and no issue had been so fiercely argued as that of slavery. Now the talking had stopped and everyone, black and white, was locked in a horrific fight to the finish. By the time it was over, more Americans had perished than in World Wars One and Two combined, $15 billion worth of property had been destroyed and vast tracts of land had been utterly devastated. African-Americans though were finally and irreversibly set free from the institutionalised slavery they had suffered for almost two hundred and fifty years.

The formal Proclamation had been made by Lincoln midway through the war, declaring that from January 1st 1863 'all persons held as slaves within any State, or designated part of the State, the people whereof shall be in rebellion against the United States, shall be then, thence forward and forever free.' Vast gatherings of slaves assembled all over America on the eve of emancipation, waiting as one group waited in a rough wooden cabin in South Carolina, where an old slave said solemnly, 'By the time I counts ten, it will be midnight and the land will be free ...' In Washington, they stood on the last night of December and sang Go Down Moses with this line added at the stroke of midnight:

> Go down Abraham, way down in Dixie's land, tell Jeff Davis, to let my people go. ❖

Photo: Author's collection.

*The young Thomas Andrew Dorsey, also known as blues singer
Georgia Tom, went on to become the Father of gospel music.*

BEEN IN THE STORM TOO LONG

Baptists, Blues and Singing Saints

"I always had rhythm in my bones. I like the solid beat. I like the long, moaning, groaning tone. I like the rock. You know how they rock and shout in the church? It's a thing people look for now."

Thomas A Dorsey was the grand old man of gospel music. No-one has had a greater influence on gospel singing; no-one has been quite as prophetic; no-one spanned the entire history of gospel music quite like Dorsey. More than any other individual, Thomas A Dorsey was gospel and his story is the cornerstone story of gospel.

In the years of reconstruction that followed the appalling carnage of the Civil War, a new generation of African-Americans was being born who would have no first hand knowledge of slavery. Dorsey was one such, delivered into a world that bitterly begrudged his parents their newly freed status and sought by all available means to reverse the events of history. The State of Georgia, like the rest of the South, was virtually running wild ... racism and bigotry of the ugliest kind ensuring that ex-slaves were confined to the 'rough side of the mountain', as church people put it. Depending on your convictions, the survival of the babe-in-arms to become the 'father of gospel' was either by very great luck or divine intervention.

Who can properly comprehend the chaos and upheaval of those terrible years in the South? Slaves had been turned loose in their hundreds of thousands - jubilation rapidly turned to terror as the first tastes of freedom soured into a frantic scramble for a subsistence income. Neither sympathy nor charity was forthcoming from white Southerners still licking the wounds of defeat - the unwilling price they paid for emancipation.

As the army of the Union poured through the Southern States, imposing a new order and authority, agencies of the Northern churches together with The Freedmen Bureau, followed quickly behind to cope in whatever ways they could with the flood of refugees. The American Missionary Society was the first in the field, having already established teaching programmes even before the Civil War. The AMS, formed in 1846, had consistently clashed with other Missionary Societies who had been more or less acquiescent towards slavery, and the progressive record of the AMS marked them out as trustworthy by ex-slaves. Ex-slave-owners on the other hand, marked them out for special attention as dangerous agitators and a number of their (mostly women) teachers were murdered or simply disappeared. By 1868, the AMS had more than five hundred teachers and ministers in the South, establishing the first black teaching and training institutions... Berea College in Kentucky, Hampton Institute in Virginia, Atlanta University in Georgia, Talladega College in Alabama, Tougaloo University in Mississippi, Straight University at New Orleans and, of course, Fisk University in Tennessee.

The extraordinary fund raising tour of the Fisk Jubilee Singers inspired many imitators, all more or less unrepresentative of the common spirituals. The Tuskagee Institute Singers were perhaps the most interesting, employing harmonic patterns which were less closely related to European conventions and which more directly preceded the styles of gospel quartets in the thirties and forties. The Pace Jubilee Singers on the other hand, were one of the first to feature a solo voice - Hattie Parker, who removed herself even further from European traditions, anticipating the vocal phrasing and surging delivery of women like Bessie Griffin and Mahalia Jackson. In the main though, the formalised attempts to present spirituals in a concert setting were solecistic, an offence to the real thing.

The AMS colleges and other similar institutions were isolated experiments in black education and advancement. As such they not only pioneered, they also divided - drawing off a narrow elite from the mass of African-Americans, to rapidly absorb all the prevailing notions of 'civilised' white behaviour. As in all else, black church music as it survived through the patronage of the AMS, is the laundered version of cultural expression. Its significance is to the outsider's perception of slave songs rather than music of black churches generally. In short, it is the sound of a myth - a myth that endures even to the present day.

In the churches, the division was acute and principally along racial lines. Before emancipation, black and white had often worshiped together, albeit within segregated confines. The camp meetings especially, offered a forum where black people shared in worship with whites, free of overt animosity. After the Civil War, however, black Christians were forced into a separatism that was almost total, reflecting the growing racial antipathies in Southern society as a whole. Apart from the fortunate few who were upwardly mobilised into white sponsored institutions, there was now minimal contact between black and white Christians and this was to have a profound effect on black religious music. In the ten years from 1860-70, the African Methodist Episcopal Zion Church grew from 20,746 members to 200,000; by 1880, the African

Methodist Episcopal Church (led by Richard Allen) was claiming 400,000 members - mostly ex-slaves. Amongst the Baptists too there was a wholesale shift to separatism. The two largest black Baptist churches: the National Baptist Convention of America and the National Baptist Convention USA, were both formed in 1880. By 1894, there were no less than 13,138 black Baptist churches and 10,119 ordained black preachers.

It is sadly ironic but undeniably a fact, that the ending of slavery also marked the beginning of black exclusion. As the writer Leroi Jones pointed out, black people in the South *'became actually isolated from the mainstream of American society ... The social repressions served to separate the Negro more effectively from his master than ever before.'* One effect of isolation was the final synthesis of English and African song traditions, shedding the constraints of the borrowed white Christian culture just as purely tribal traditions of Africa had already been forcibly shed, thereby creating a truly African-American form of worship.

Behind the political scenes, shady deals were being struck which would further deepen the racial divisions and conspire to re-impose servitude on black people. In order to negotiate a measure of civil order into the frightening social chaos, the Northern army of occupation conceded the 'right' of Southerners to inflict a vast range of punitive restrictions on the already impoverished and beleaguered 'freedmen'. In 1876, the last of the Federal troops were withdrawn, having received spurious assurances that the civil rights of black people would be respected. It was like leaving a fox in charge of a hen-house; within a matter of months, Southerners had secured an authority over black workers almost indistinguishable from the slave-owning conspiracies of two decades earlier. Men and women weren't sold on the auction block any more - just their homes, their crops, their tools, their food, their clothes, their every means to life. Just as before, they bent their backs twelve or fourteen hours a day in the burning sun for a master, only now they had a choice: this or starvation. In many ways it was worse than slavery - at least then there was the minimal provision of the basic elements of survival: food and shelter. Now it was clear that four million slaves had made the journey out of Egypt, only for deliverance into serfdom. The people freed were entrapped as sharecroppers as surely as they had been by slavery.

Many fled the farms and rural areas, looking for work in New Orleans, Memphis, Mobile and Savannah - big bustling ports and expanding industrial centres. They loaded ships and sweated in cotton and steel mills, living packed into ghettoes and company shacks. Surprisingly, few fled North - the great migrations didn't come until much later - and in 1880, three-quarters of all African-Americans were still living in the South. The introduction of the infamous Segregation Statutes (the so-called Jim Crow laws) in the later part of the 1880s, set the seal on the fate of African-Americans, consigning them to legally enforceable positions of inferiority. The Statutes successfully achieved their intention to maintain and, where possible, extend white supremacy.

Black music and black religion had been virtually inseparable until now, with spirituals dominating almost completely the song forms of African-Americans. Even the work songs were often spirituals re-worked for the purpose. The first ever collection of black folk music, *Slave Songs of the United States*, published soon after the Civil War, was made up almost entirely of spirituals and these songs continued to pre-occupy black folk culture for the rest of the century.

However, by the time Thomas Dorsey was born (on July 1st 1899), the first notes of a new kind of music were coming to be heard - the blues. Nobody quite knows how they began or where, but they coincided with an increasing social mobility and the rise of secular individualism - an ethic of lone survival in desperate circumstances. Whereas the music of the black church was almost entirely choral and communal, the blues were usually voiced by solo singers. One man or one woman telling a story and scraping a living - occasionally even a spectacular living. Blues singer Bill Broonzy, who was born in Mississippi in 1893, recalled that the first popular bluesmen were known as 'sweet black papas' and tasted the forbidden fruit:

> *"Them men didn't know how cotton and corn and rice and sugar-cane grows and they didn't care. They went out, dressed up every night and some of them had three or four women. One fed him and the other bought his clothes and shoes. These is the men that wear ten-dollar Stetson hats and twenty-dollar gold pieces at their watch and diamonds in their teeth and on their fingers."*

The ostentatious exception was rarely the rule but, in that they articulated emotional suffering and material desires common to many, blues singers were in this and other ways setting themselves apart and coming to assume the role of secular spokesmen and women. As such, they implicitly challenged the position of the church minister, and the blues implicitly challenged the consolatory function of the spiritual. The one quickly became anathema to the other, but in musical form at least the two musics weren't so dissimilar: *"When you hear people singing hymns in church - these long, drawn out songs - that's the blues. Church music and the blues is all one and the same. They come out of the same soul, same heart, same body,"* declared bluesman Johnny Shines. Or as singer T. Bone Walker put it,

> *"Of course, the blues come a lot from the church, too. The first time I ever heard a boogie-woogie piano was the first time I went to church. That was the Holy Ghost church in Dallas, Texas. That boogie-woogie was a kind of blues, I guess. The preacher used to preach in a bluesy tone sometimes. You even got the congregation yelling 'Amen' all the time when his preaching would stir them up - his preaching and the bluesy tone."*

And again: *"The blues? Why the blues are part of me,"* said Alberta Hunter. *"To me, the blues are - well almost religious. They're like a chant. The blues are like spirituals, almost sacred. When we sing blues, we're singin' out our hearts, we're singin' out our feelings. Maybe we're hurt and just can't answer back, then we sing or maybe even hum the blues. Yes, to us, the blues are sacred."* In fact so many singers of the period testify to the correlation between sacred and profane songs that it seems that one must often have been a parody of the other. Some blues singers seem happy to own up to it ... *"The blues ain't nothing but a steal from the spirituals,"* was the cheerful admission of one.

The use of the world 'blues' to describe a mood of sadness goes back to Elizabethan times and it was known as a slang expression in America during the 19th century. But veteran pianist Harrison Barnes remembered that the music came first, the name-tag later: *"They was slow tunes, unhappy. They was what they call blues now, only they called them ditties in them days."* Rev Ledell Johnson, who was born in Mississippi in 1892, recalled that his uncle George had 'an old hobby-horse outfit' of a band and that he *"... didn't know nothing about these blues. He played these little old love songs ... see they had these little jump-up songs ... the little old blues they had to my idea wasn't worth fifteen cents."*

Whatever their value, the blues caught on, and so did another new sound born about the same time. Down in New Orleans, Buddy Bolden was putting together the first jazz band in a dance pavilion in 1895. Needless to say, neither form of music celebrated clean living, sobriety or sexual restraint and they were very soon a heresy to upright black church folk who saw in them an increasingly popular inducement to despair. Lil Son Jackson quit blues for the church and told it this way:

"You see it's two different things - the blues and church songs is two different things. If a man feel hurt within side and he sing a church song then he's askin' God for help ... but I think if a man sings the blues it's more or less out of himself, if you know what I mean, see. He's not askin' no one for help. And he's not really clinging to no one. But he's expressin' how he feel. He's expressin' it to someone and that fact makes it a sin you know, because it make another man sin. Make another woman sin."

The blues took its quota of sinners and the black church defiantly held to its saints. They were the two most powerful spheres of cultural influence and Thomas A. Dorsey grew up feeling the urgent pull of them both. The Baptist church was the denomination that commanded greatest support amongst ex-slaves, its various liturgical traditions of water immersion and spirit possession allowing *'Africans and their descendants to behave in what to them were the proper ways of expressing worship.'* As father of the blues W.C. Handy remembered from his childhood:

"The Baptists had no organ in their church and no choir. They didn't need any. The lusty singers sat in the amen corner and raised the songs, raised them as they were intended to be raised, if I'm any judge. None of the dressed-up arrangements one sometimes hears on the concert stage for them. They knew a better way. Theirs was pure rhythm. While critics like to describe their numbers as shouting songs, rhythm was their basic element. And rhythm was the thing that drew me and other members of our home town quartet to attend the Baptist services."

Rev T. M. Dorsey was a country Baptist preacher of the old school, raising his son on Dr Watts' hymns, personal salvation and that pure Baptist rhythm. As a boy in rural Georgia, Thomas had an irrepressible urge to be a musician and he determined to learn the piano, walking more than thirty miles a week to and from Mrs Graves' music lessons. *"She was the only music teacher who taught the black folk at that time."* Father approved the diligence but not the performing ambitions, sensing the lure of the stage in the boy. Old man Dorsey was right. Thomas was a child prodigy and wormed his way into show-business by any back door open to him. As a boy he worked for a local circus, fetching and carrying water and doing little errands. He remembered a big evangelical revival held in the circus tent, squeezing his way in on 'coloured night' to hear Calvin P. Dixon (nicknamed Black Billy Sunday). *"When he got hot, he'd take off his coat and loosen his collar and everyone would holler Amen and Hallelujah. It must have just been a gesture but the people went wild."*

Even before he was a teenager, Thomas was gaining something of a reputation locally as a fair blues pianist and, within a few years, was playing for Saturday night dances and sometimes getting paid for it. How his father viewed his dalliance with the 'devil's music' isn't on record, but there were rather more pressing concerns to worry about. Dorsey Senior had been working on a farm at Villa Rica *'for forty or fifty cents a day'*, struggling to support his family as well as discharge his duties as a minister. Like thousands of others

35

Photo: Author's collection.

*Thomas Dorsey playing piano with
Ma Rainey and her Wildcat band. c.1925*

he found the struggle too much and eventually quit, moving the family to Atlanta where there were infinitely better work prospects. With the work came the money and the nightlife. Decatur Street was full of it all and the 81 Theatre was the showplace, sandwiched between the pool-hall and the barber shop. Soon after arriving in Atlanta, Thomas found work and an education of sorts there:

"As a boy I sold pop, ginger ale, red rock at the 81 Theatre. And I got a chance to meet all the stars, all of the performers that came to the theatre. And there they'd want a pop or something, a cold drink on credit until payday, and I got a chance to know them all! I stayed round that theatre, I'd hang around the theatre and I learned a lot. And I learned blues, I could play piano, and I think it paid off very well to me."'

The theatre and the street were run by gangsters Handsome Harry, Lucky Sambo and Joe Slocum ...

"They controlled all the wild bar rooms which started rolling at 5 a.m. and closed at midnight. Any one who knew their way around could always get a belly-full of corn whiskey at Walter Harrison's, Henry Thomas' and Lonnie Reid's joint until daybreak. It was a tame Saturday night in the notorious Decatur Street section if there were only six razor operations performed or if only four persons were found in the morgue on Sunday morning."

The city stood on a commercial crossroads, linking the Deep South with the big northern and eastern cities. White workers in Atlanta were fiercely hostile to the influx of black migrants from rural areas and the town erupted in serious race riots in 1906. Uneasy truces prevailed, but by 1915 the Ku Klux Klan was once again in business, holding mass 'Klonventions' on Stone Mountain overlooking the town. Thomas could recall the tension but preferred not to:

"I try to forget it. It was nasty as far as I'm concerned. There was a feeling someone was pressing, eventually to make the financial gain, that the black man wouldn't get a chance to do so well financially. Down there, in small towns there, if a white man came walking down the street and it was a narrow path, I'd have to get out and let him pass."

At the same time he'd also talk with obvious pleasure of childhood friendships with white boys living across the road: *"Nobody bothered us, they came to my house and played with me. I ain't never had trouble with black and white, I can get these special vibrations just coming into a room and they keep me from troubles."*

Whether directly as a consequence of the Klan revival or not, Dorsey left Atlanta the following year and joined the great migrations northward. He was just seventeen and his head was overflowing with the conflicting sounds of church and barrelhouse. His years in Atlanta had been spent immersed in both blues and spirituals and he moved shamelessly between one world and the other, reluctant to fully accept either's claim on his talents.

He'd rubbed shoulders with some of the classic blues names like Bessie Smith, who he heard as early as 1912, and the legendary Ma Rainey. Rainey was some thirteen years older than Thomas and distinctly outrageous, both in public and in private. She came from nearby Columbus, but was known throughout the southern entertainment circuit as the most formidable blues shouter, performing for a time with the

Rabbit Foot Minstrels and then with her husband as *'Rainey and Rainey, the Assassinators of the Blues'*. Thomas was spell-bound. This was heady stuff for a young Baptist boy, but it wasn't until the late 1920s that he finally got to work with Ma Rainey. Ethel Waters too was around the Atlanta circuit, performing *St Louis Blues* to Bessie Smith audiences, so the secular attractions in Dorsey's home town were really something quite special.

On the other side of the fence though, he had also associated with the new breed of church preachers and singers like the 'Famous Georgia Peach', otherwise known as Clara Hudmon, someone whom Dorsey always maintained was the even match of a Bessie Smith; and the amazing Rev J.M.Gates, who went on to become the first really big selling black recording artist, with a series of hair-raising sermonettes.

Records, incidentally, were a whole new medium that had just begun to open up. In 1903, the very first recordings of any kind of black music anywhere in the world were issued by Victor Talking Machine Records. They featured the 'genuine Jubilee and Camp Meeting Shouts' of the Dinwiddie Coloured Quartet. Surprisingly perhaps, those first six recordings lived up to their claims, displaying none of the cloying sentimentality and concert hall pretensions of other early groups like the Pace and Fisk Jubilee Singers. However, interminable patent disputes put a freeze on the new industry and no other black music appeared on record for at least eighteen years.

Elsewhere in the State of Georgia, another of the great gospel pioneers was growing up under the same sweltering oppressions as the Dorsey family. A young Sallie Martin had moved into Atlanta from the little hamlet of Pittfield around the same time as the Dorsey family, but, though she and Dorsey were later to team up in Chicago and revolutionise church music, they never met on home territory. Like Dorsey, Sallie was brought up as a Baptist but switched to the Fire Baptised Holiness sect in 1916. The Holiness or Sanctified Churches (the so-called Holy Rollers) were springing up all over the South, some calling on pentecostal fire, others - the Latter Rain churches - on a spiritual down-pour.

Sallie's commitment to the Holiness church was absolute. She heard the blues but she didn't care to listen. Her music was all Holiness music, ecstatic and extempore: *"We didn't have no soloists. We would all sing together or if you felt like you were going to testify, you might start out with a song yourself."* To shout or fall out when the spirit hits you is an impulse intrinsic to real gospel, a continuous thread running through the full span of the music from camp meeting spirituals right up to the modern soul-stirrings of the Clark Sisters and Kirk Franklin. Musicologists and historians argue over whether the shout and the 'holy dance' are rooted in African spiritual traditions or are borrowed from the charismatic outpourings of 19th century Christianity. The truth is likely to be that they are simply further evidence of the synthesis of the two.

An academic issue of course for Sallie Martin, taking such Holiness fervour and spontaneity with her as she travelled from Atlanta, first to Cleveland and then up to Chicago. Thomas Dorsey made the same journey to the same city - only he went via Indiana and arrived with the blues and spirituals of Georgia. They weren't to meet up until sixteen years later.

With the First World War in full swing, heavy industry in the North boomed and European immigration slumped. The subsequent labour famine enticed hundreds of thousands of African-Americans from sharecropping poverty to a relative prosperity in the new ghettoes. The black population of Chicago between 1910 and 1920 increased by one and a half times; in Detroit it was even more dramatic - up six-fold. In all the big northern industrial centres, vast numbers of new city folk were picking up regular wages in the steel mills, the stockyards, the foundries and the packing houses. *"We went looking for money, man, good money,"* says Dorsey, just one of the more than 50,000 southern migrants who arrived in Chicago between 1915 and 1919.

They mostly travelled with more than just the hope of good money though. The North had always beckoned as a refuge from the rigours of slavery and now it also held out an imagined hope for racial justice. One Mississippi preacher told the US Department for Labour enquiry into the migration:

> *"My father was born and brought up as a slave. He never knew anything else until after I was born. He was taught his place and was content to keep it. But when he brought me up he let some of the old customs slip by. But I know there are certain things that I must do and I do them, and it doesn't worry me; yet in bringing up my own son, I let some more of the old customs slip by ... He says, 'When a young white talks rough to me, I can't talk rough to him. You can stand that - I can't. I have some education and inside I has the feelings of a white man. I'm going.'"*

If the preacher's son was going North in search of justice, then the reality must have been a terrible shock. Savage race riots consumed the major cities. Over a seven month period in 1919 there were twenty-five serious race riots led by white vigilante gangs. The worst was in Chicago itself when twenty-three black people were killed, 600 wounded and a thousand families burned out. During the next four years, more than fifty black homes were dynamited. *"I came here looking for deliverance,"* said Dorsey without irony or bitterness, *"And to get deliverance you just have to wait on the movements of providence."*

Twenty-two years old then and still a barrelhouse piano player, Dorsey wasn't slow either in re-locating his spiritual roots. He joined the Pilgrim Baptist Church of Chicago and began writing a few church songs, though more out of curiosity than from any burning conviction.

He didn't really get himself properly converted until the summer of that year, when the (all black) National Baptist Convention met at Pilgrim. One of the great extrovert singer-preachers of the time was Rev A. W. Nix, who set the convention alight with his performance of *I Do, Don't You?*

> *"He was great! He was powerful! He rocked that convention: shouts, moans, hollers, screaming. I said to myself, 'That's what I want to do. That's good gospel, and I want to be a gospel singer!' That's where I first got the gospel word, and I was converted at that meeting. I wrote a song then and there, that week, for the Gospel Pearl, a song book which may still be distributed by the Baptist Convention. It's on page 119. I never got any royalties for it, I just let them have it."*

The singer (and the song) that saved Thomas Dorsey, is of more than casual interest. Rev Nix was a shouting preacher in the mould of Rev J.M. Gates, back in Atlanta. His big number, famed throughout America, was the *Black Diamond Express To Hell* - a typically bombastic sermonette that left little to the imagination. Vocalion Records issued it a few years later, with an advert full of glee and relish:

Top (L): The first great African-American spiritual composer, Rev Charles Albert Tindley. (R): Lucie Campbell.
Below (L): The only known likeness of Arizona Dranes. (R): The phenomenal Rev J. M. Gates.

Photo: Chris Strachwitz

Street preaching and singing. Rev Louis Overstreet and his sons from St Luke's
Powerhouse Church of God in Christ, Phoenix, Arizona, 1962

'Here she comes! The Black Diamond Express To Hell, with Sin the Engineer, holding the throttle wide open; Pleasure is the Headlight, and the Devil is the Conductor. You can feel the roaring of the Express and the moanin' of the Drunkards, Liars, Gamblers and other folks who have got aboard. They are hell-bound and they don't want to go. The train makes eleven stops but nobody can get off ...'

Gates himself had a similar sermon - *Death's Black Train Is Coming* - and both were massive sellers in the so-called 'race market', far out-stripping sales by big secular names like Bessie Smith. Recordings like these, which are now widely available on re-issue labels, provide us with a taste of the prevailing atmosphere that encompassed all the extremes of showbusiness melodrama and religious ecstasy.

Nix's style that night at the 1921 Convention however was slightly more sombre. The song he sang that so galvanised Dorsey is often wrongly credited to another hugely influential figure of the period - Dr Charles Albert Tindley. More than anyone else though, Tindley is the man who inspired Dorsey to become a gospel songwriter, and the best of the Tindley songs have endured right through to contemporary gospel, just like the Watts' hymns. The Staple Singers in the 1960s turned in a definitively passionate version of one of his greatest compositions, *Stand By Me*, Mavis Staples paring the beautiful economy of the song even further by using only the first verse:

> *When the storms of life are raging,*
> *Stand by me.*
> *When the world is tossing me*
> *Like a ship upon the sea,*
> *Thou who rulest wind and water,*
> *Stand by me.*

Charles Albert Tindley was born of slave parents in Maryland on 7th July 1856. From as early as he could remember he was obsessed with the idea of education, collecting scraps of newspaper found on the roadside and painstakingly deciphering the words late at night by the light of the fire. In this way he gradually taught himself to read and he became known locally as the 'boy with the bare feet who could read the Bible'.

By the time he was seventeen, his self-education had been so successful that he could read and write fluently. He met and fell in love with Daisy Henry and the young couple moved north to Philadelphia, where he picked up work first as a hod carrier, then as sexton at the Bainbridge Street Methodist Episcopal Church - continuing his studies at evening classes. In 1885, Tindley became a church minister and spent the next seventeen years as an itinerant pastor, returning finally to take charge of the same Bainbridge Street church he'd originally joined as a menial. Here he remained until his death in 1933, loved and respected by the community to the extent that they later renamed the church Tindley Temple.

Renowned during his lifetime as an eloquent preacher, Tindley is best remembered now as a pre-gospel hymn writer. In his church at Bainbridge Street he combined both talents to great effect by interspersing vivid sermons with choruses and songs he'd written himself. With the congregation joining in under his direction, a form of worship developed which became known during the 1950s as a 'gospel songfest'.

Tindley was writing from 1901 onwards and must be credited with being the earliest to combine blues formats and moods with great hymn themes and spirituals. His was an entirely new genre in religious song - directly in the tradition of Dr Watts but employing black folk imagery, distinctly innovative and African-American, but not yet gospel music as it would soon become. *"There were no gospel songs then, we called them evangelistic songs,"* Dorsey pointed out, but the distinctions are often just semantics to the outsider. Who can really say for instance, that Tindley's *Storm Is Passing Over* isn't gospel in the hands of Marie Knight or *We'll Understand It Better By And By* as performed by Roberta Martin or *Leave It There* by Washington Phillips. Still less, who could categorise the Tindley song that was adapted first as a civil rights theme song and then elevated to the status of a trans-national protest anthem:

I'll overcome, I'll overcome, I'll overcome some day,
If in my life I do not yield, I'll overcome some day.

Tindley's greatest strength lay in knowing his people - for them he created a form of strong, emotive worship, skilfully supported by simple yet tuneful melodies and harmonies. His songs fall into two main groups. One of his favourite methods of composing was to take a passage from the Bible and re-word it in unembellished, everyday language. The other favoured method was to tell a story or describe a situation in the form of a song - the story-line is established in the first verse and the theme continued throughout, frequently upheld by a strong moral element.

He also differed in many respects from his songwriting predecessors in that he concentrated on the plight and troubles of black Christians in the 20th century, as well as the joys of the after-life. Previously emphasis had been placed on salvation and conversion with very little recognition of the hardships of everyday life. Musically, Tindley was a great advocate of cheerful tunes, which were easily learnt and enabled the congregation to join in with great abandon. Most of his melodies are based on the popular pentatonic scale and allow a great deal of room to manoeuvre in terms of improvisation and interpretation, knowing as he did that spiritual gospel music is as much a creation of the singer, as the composer.

Dr C.A. Tindley published a collection of his hymns and songs in Philadelphia in 1916 under the singularly appropriate title *New Songs of Paradise*. Five years later came the publication of a hymn-book called *Gospel Pearls* aimed specifically at black churchgoers. It paid tribute to Tindley's skill as a composer by including six of his songs. One of those involved in the selection of titles for the hymnal was Lucie Eddie Campbell Williams (1885-1963), a noted Baptist song-writer herself and greatly influenced by Tindley's work. Lucie Campbell takes pride of place as the first black female gospel composer and, along with Tindley and Dorsey, is revered as one of the great early pioneers in the field. The daughter of former slave parents from Duck Hill, Mississippi, Lucie wrote over eighty songs, several of which have become classics in the world of gospel. Numbered among them are *Jesus Gave Me Water*, beautifully rendered by the Soul Stirrers and the Davis Sisters and *In The Upper Room With Jesus* made famous by Mahalia Jackson.

The story of Thomas Dorsey and the birth of gospel music should really proceed logically from here; but it doesn't. In fact, Dorsey returned to the secular blues world in the early 20s to carve out a highly successful career under the name of Georgia Tom. A chance had come up for him to join Ma Rainey again, up from Atlanta and riding exceptionally high as Paramount's biggest selling star.

Top (L): Azuza Street, Los Angeles, 1906, birthplace of Pentecostalism; (R): Church of God in Christ founding Bishop Charles Mason. Below: An early Holiness church

Photos: Author's collection/Library of Congress.

It's tempting, but facile, to cast Dorsey at this point as an opportunist and a back-slider. He was a musician by trade and blues offered a good living, just as a brick-layer might be building houses while nursing a greater ambition to build churches. The Baptists didn't quite see it that way, but Dorsey was thoroughly unashamed of his early secular career and of course there's no reason why he shouldn't be. After all, it was his formative experience as a bluesman and entertainer that was to give gospel music its distinctive qualities in the first place.

Towards the end of his life, old Thomas looked back with evident fondness to his days with Ma Rainey and her Wildcat Band:

> "She was one of the loveliest people I ever worked for or worked with. She called everybody 'honey' and 'darling', 'baby' and so on. If you got in trouble and wanted to borrow money or something from her, and you go to her for it, she wouldn't call you 'darling', 'babe' or 'baby'! She said, 'What did you do with your money? All right, here it is ...' She was that kind of person."

As Georgia Tom, he composed many of Ma Rainey's hits, giving them a sleazy mystique that is difficult to equate with Dorsey's later career as a gospel writer. He chuckled over the contradictions and, with only the merest hint of embarrassment, described the songs as "... deep moanin', low-down blues, that's all I could say!" Rainey certainly had her influence on Dorsey but there's a good chance that it wasn't all one-way and in fact, towards the end of her life she returned to Georgia and became deeply committed to the Congregation of Friendship Baptist Church, where her brother was a deacon. On her death certificate in 1939, Ma Rainey's occupation was entered as 'housekeeping'.

Marriage (to Nettie Harper in 1925) brought Thomas back into the church but it was another brief sojourn. He teamed up with guitarist Hudson Whittaker (known as Tampa Red, for his Florida origins) and the duo proceeded to scandalise the churches with their 1928 recording of the highly erotic It's Tight Like That, released by Vocalion. In the burgeoning 'race' market it was an instant smash hit, spawning dozens of imitators and earning Dorsey an astounding first royalty cheque of $2,400. It also earned for him the opprobrium of the churches and, even now, as Dorsey comes to be revered in gospel history almost as a saint, this episode in his life is sometimes conveniently glossed over. It's not difficult to see why he was ostracised a couple of years later when he tried to sell his new kind of gospel music to the churches.

Despite his great commercial success however, Dorsey was experiencing an undercurrent of dissatisfaction with his life as Georgia Tom. His partner Tampa Red noticed a sudden coolness in him as they travelled to New York to record a follow-up for Vocalion. He recalled that Tom was '.. very smart', wearing his best suit and carrying a brief-case that he kept on the floor beside him as he played. Tampa guessed something was up when Dorsey skipped the usual post-recording drinks party. He was to learn later that Thomas's brief-case was stuffed full of promotional material for some new religious songs he'd been writing, and that the afternoon had been spent visiting churches and choir directors in New York.

Tampa Red rarely saw him after that final recording and, despite some speculation that he continued recording blues under the pseudonym 'Black Bob', Dorsey committed himself exclusively to a gospel music ministry from 1929 onwards.

Throughout the 1920s, African-American church music was characterised by four distinct styles. Firstly, by the jubilee singing groups who held to the traditional styles of spirituals and jubilee songs; secondly, by the many singing preachers who built large followings with their sermons and hymns; thirdly, by the itinerant street evangelists, often self-accompanied on guitar in rural blues fashion; and finally by the Sanctified singers and musicians of the Holiness churches, of whom Arizona Dranes and Bessie Johnson are perhaps the best known, combining hymns and ragtime in a heady mix. The whole of this decade is important because of the advent of recording on a commercial scale. The long years of patent disputes that followed the Dinwiddie Colored Quartet records in 1903 were over and the new record companies were eager to exploit the untapped 'race' market.

Set against a background of intense racist activity (the Ku Klux Klan were once again running riot, with an estimated four million members), African-American religious music was being sold into homes as a commercial product for the first time. The Paramount Records catalogue in 1924 was offering heavy shellac recordings (at 78 rpm) of their most popular male group, the Norfolk Jubilee Quartet, led by Norman 'Crip' Harris. (In 1969, long after the Quartet stopped recording, the totally blind Harris was murdered by thugs in New York). Paramount were one of the earliest companies in the field and even sponsored their own Paramount Jubilee Singers, but the most interesting item offered for sale in that catalogue is the first recording of the great Tindley song *Stand By Me*.

There were some early attempts to set up black-owned record companies but they didn't last long. One such was Meritt Records owned by Winston Holmes, who recorded sermons by Rev H.C. Gatewood and Rev J.C. Burnett, who had great success with his *Downfall Of Nebuchadnezzar* and *I've Even Heard Of Thee*. Shortly after, Columbia Records moved in, snapped up Burnett and put Holmes out of business. It was no consolation to Holmes that his experience set a historical precedent.

Columbia were the second major company into the market place. In 1926 they sent a field unit down to Atlanta where they recorded the Birmingham Jubilee Singers and also discovered the famous Rev J.M. Gates. The Birmingham Jubilee Singers' first record was *He Took My Sins Away* and *Crying To The Lord* and it sold almost 5,000 copies. Their second did even better, selling 13,000 copies and establishing them as the first big recording name in the quartet style.

The most significant find for Columbia however was the magniloquent Rev Gates, and on that first Atlanta session they recorded four of his 'sermons with singing'. On *Death's Black Train Is Coming*, Gates is joined by two female members of his congregation and declares: *"I want to sing a song tonight, and while I sing I want every sinner in the house to come to the angel's feet and bow and accept prayer - you need prayer. Subject of this song, Death's Black Train Is Coming - it's coming too."* Somehow the engineers had managed to get a train whistle to blow in the background and the band of singers launch into dire warnings of the railroad to hell. As the first sermons on record to feature singing, the Atlanta recordings were a sensational success, and when the remaining two sides were issued in October 1926, the advance order alone was a massive 34,025 copies.

Rev J. M. Gates was quite a star but somehow he escaped contractual ties to Columbia and worked for as many as six different labels, recording an astonishing forty-two sides within the space of three weeks. He

Early pre-war quartets. Top: Mitchell's Christian Singers.
Below: The Utica Jubilee Quartet.

loved to put dramatic and topical titles to his records and would preach sermons like *Tiger Flower's Last Fight*, *God's Wrath In The St Louis Cyclone*, *Hitler And Hell*, or *Will Hell Be Your Santa Claus*. He influenced just about every other singer-preacher and many of them, like Rev H. R. Tomlin, Rev W. M. Mosley and Rev Moses Doolittle were signed up by record companies. During a single nine month period (from September 1926 to June 1927) sixty records of sermons were put out by the various companies - no less than forty of them by Rev J. M. Gates.

More companies moved into the market. The Victor catalogue of 1929 has some old recordings of the Taskiana Four and the Pace Jubilee Singers, as well as sermons by Rev F. W. McGee, Rev E. D. Campbell and Rev Gates himself. McGee is interesting as an example of the new instrumental groups that appeared in Holiness churches in the late twenties. This was a controversial move and condemned by many black churches as irreligious but the music is joyous in the extreme. Rev McGee's *Fifty Miles Of Elbow Room* features a jazz band with the congregation and his recording in Detroit in 1929 of *Jesus The Lord Is A Saviour* sounds like an enthusiastic amateur jazz orchestra doing a Sunday School chorus.

Of all the great preachers in the 'sermon boom' though, Gates remains the most important and most influential representative of the music that was typical in churches at the time. Amongst collectors today, original copies of Rev Gates' 78s are as eagerly sought-after as old Bessie Smith records.

The itinerant guitar-playing evangelists were meanwhile also getting their chance to record; the first being Blind Joe Taggart in 1926 singing *Take Your Burden To The Lord* and *Just Beyond Jordan* followed later that year by Rev E. W. Clayborn. Clayborn was a strident country blues singer who also played 'a singing bottle-neck guitar' and his first record for Vocalion was *The Gospel Train is Coming* backed by *Your Enemy Cannot Harm You (But Watch Your Close Friend)*. When first issued, the record was listed only as being by 'The Guitar Evangelist' but they were highly popular and later pressings gave Clayborn proper credit.

A year later, Columbia took a field unit to Dallas and Memphis and recorded two of the great religious singers of the South: Washington Phillips, who was noted for playing a curious instrument called the dulceola, and a singer much revered by blues collectors: Blind Willie Johnson.

Johnson was a Texas farm boy, blinded at seven by his stepmother during a domestic fight. With few options other than to beg for a living, he became a kind of religious busker, standing in the streets of Marlin, Hearn and Dallas with a tin cup tied to the neck of a battered guitar. In 1927 the tall, gangling twenty-five year old with a thin moustache married Angeline, who taught him many of the songs he became famous for. Most of them came from old songbooks she kept in a trunk in the back of their house, like the *Redeemer's Praise, For Sunday School, Church And Family* by T. C. Okane, published in 1881.

Blind Willie Johnson's records - thirty in all - are intense and moving testimonies sung in a tortured, rasping voice over his visceral guitar style, often switching their functions at the end of a line for dramatic effect. The first record, issued in the last week of January 1928, was *I Know His Blood Can Make Me Whole* and *Jesus Make Up My Dying Bed*, advertised by Columbia as 'The new sensation in the singing of sacred songs - and what guitar accompaniment!'

Photos: Author's Collection/Roy Francis.

Guitar evangelists. Top: Elder Utah Smith (L); Blind Willie Johnson (R). Below: One of the last surviving practitioners, Rev Anderson Johnson at home in Newport News, Virginia, 1995.

Those recordings were timeless works of folk art and Blind Willie Johnson has become at least as mythologically significant to gospel blues as Robert Johnson is to the secular variety.

The success of the records made little difference to Willie's life. He never got more than a few dollars from the company and he remained a street beggar all his life. Even in the late 1940s, when his name had become a legend among sophisticated jazz collectors, he was still living in obscurity down in rural Texas. After putting out a fire in his house one night in 1949, Angeline lay newspapers over the wet bedding and they were both soaked and cold by morning. Standing out in the winter winds the next day, singing to earn a little money, Willie got sick and within a few days was dying of pneumonia. When Angeline took him to hospital he wasn't admitted. *"They wouldn't accept him. He'd be living today if they'd accepted him. They wouldn't accept him because he was blind. Blind folks has a hard time ..."*

During the late 1920s, itinerant evangelists were selling so well on record that even secular bluesmen like Blind Lemon Jefferson were putting out religious items ... in his case under the pseudonym 'Deacon L. J. Bates'. A few guitar evangelists, like Rev Anderson Johnson (famous for his 50s recording *God Don't Like It*) and Bishop Manning in North Carolina, survive into the present day.

But the great recording successes of the 20s were the preachers, and in the peak year of 1926, Rev J. C. Burnett's re-recording of *Downfall of Nebuchadnezzar* sold a staggering 80,000 copies soon after its release. A measure of its popularity is that the best-selling blues artist of the time, Bessie Smith, could only manage a quarter of that figure. But perhaps the best known popular sermon of the whole decade was the *Black Diamond Express To Hell* by the Rev A. W. Nix, the man who can take the credit for singing so powerfully at the National Baptist Convention that he turned the heart of a certain Thomas A. Dorsey to gospel singing....

> *"This rhythm I had, I brought with me to gospel songs. I was a blues singer, and I carried that with me into the gospel songs. These songs were not just written. Something had to happen, something had to be done, there had to be a feeling. They weren't just printed and distributed. Somebody had to feel something, someone had to hand down light for mankind's pathway, smooth the road and the rugged way, give him courage, bring the Black man peace, joy and happiness. Gospel songs come from prayer, meditation, hard times and pain. But they are written out of divine memories, out of the feelings in your soul."* ❖

LET THE CHURCH ROLL ON

Mr Dorsey and the Gospel Mothers

Thomas Dorsey's way with gospel music started a revolution. It upset the spirituals and it upset the people who sang them. African-American styles of worship may have been from the beginning infinitely more exuberant than white, but it doesn't follow that the black churches are any the more receptive to radical changes in direction. At best it's an instinct for survival, a defensive closing of ranks against an external threat. Black-led churches in white-run societies don't often have the wealth or the power of their established counterparts. They tend to be communities of the common people with a superhuman ability to carve out places of worship in the hostile city rocks, against all the odds. They know about the hard sweat that goes into real miracles. Every brick, every song book, every choir robe has been bought and is maintained year by year from tithes and donations that come gladly out of wage packets that contained precious little in the first place. The elders and the mothers didn't build Sunday-only churches, they built a community of worship - a sacred household living in constant danger of eviction and exploitation. In many cases the household faced actual physical attack and desecration.

Not surprisingly, African-American church leaders were (and still are) tenacious defenders of the faithful as well as of the faith. By the same token though, they're often extremely conservative, regarding internal pressures for change with a similar defensiveness and suspicion. It's one reason for the astonishing proliferation of different doctrines and churches - it being easier for dissidents to launch new denominations than to effect reform from within. Even today, in gospel churches on both sides of the Atlantic, one pastor's righteousness is another's schism.

Nowhere is this intransigence more apparent than in styles of worship, where faith is demonstrated in tangible form in a manner that is familiar and comforting to the elders of the church. Even in the Pentecostal churches, where the worship is subordinate to the movement of the Holy Spirit, there is nevertheless a hierarchy and a culture that will dictate the form of a service as much as any Liturgical Commission would for Roman Catholics. Perhaps it's only human nature that an omnipotent and unchanging God should inspire a hundred different, and equally immutable, forms of worship.

Small wonder then that the churches most definitely did not take kindly to the attentions of a famous barrelhouse bluesman and his new line in 'gospel' songs. However much Dorsey tried to smarten himself up and exploit his old Baptist connections, he was still the ignominious 'Georgia Tom' who'd made his name with Ma Rainey and Tampa Red, the man who'd co-written the erotic smash hit of the decade. Not only that, he was trying to bring all that blues stuff and mix it with the spirituals, with the Tindley and the Watts hymns. He had hawked his songs round to ministers and he had mailed out hundreds of copies to churches all round the country but the response was predictable:

> *"I'll tell you how it happened. I had about $13 in the bank, and I had to spend that. I got addresses of missions from a magazine of the National Baptist Convention. I borrowed $5 and got 250 two cent stamps (you could mail a letter for that much then). I put the songs in the mail and sent them off to the churches. What do you think happened? Nothing! Do you know it was a year and nine months before I got a reply?"* Looking back to that time, there was a rare trace of bitterness in his voice: *"I got thrown out of some of the best churches in them days. If they'd been good ministerial men they would have helped me ... I felt like going back to the jazz field of music. Many times I walked through the snow from church to church until my feet were soaked ... I was very thankful to God for a good day when I had a dollar and a half in my pocket to take home to Nellie."*

The year it all started to happen for Dorsey and for gospel music was 1932. In a matter of a few months, a confluence of events began to turn the whole of black church music upside down.

The supplanting of spirituals by gospel songs was a major controversy within the churches and, though we can now take it for granted that the two music forms are part of one continuum, the introduction of Dorsey's gospel songs incited great antagonism. From the earliest moan to the latest digitally recorded melisma, spiritual and gospel music together can be considered to have a history spanning about two-and-a-half centuries, but only the last sixty five years really belong to gospel.

Gospel music was perceived then to be the great usurper, the jazzed-up two-cents parody of Christian music, the defiler of sacred hymnody with downhome blues, the sweet sounds of heaven thrown together with the noise of hell. Preachers throughout America would try to force it back, but the weight of two hundred years of African-American church music tipped over into gospel in the space of this one year.

Thomas A. Dorsey wasn't so much the founder of gospel music - that's a convenient piece of mythologising - but he was certainly its major catalyst. He tipped the balance in 1932 but only because an extraordinary pattern of events allowed him to. He was an ordinary person with a particular talent and a vision of how best to use it, but he also had the advantage of being in exactly the right place at the right time. The place being Chicago and the time ... the Great Depression of the 1930s.

"I don't know what brought on the Depression," he would say with a quick shake of his head, *"I don't know. I didn't feel so depressed for I didn't have a thing to start with."* When it began with the Wall Street Crash in 1929, Dorsey was still outside the church and, as earnings tumbled and rents trebled, he was kept busy, though not rich, playing piano at 'rent parties'.

> *"I had a circuit, I had a place to play every night. If you got 50 cents, or 35 cents a night for playing piano for three or four hours you had good money. They'd have to raise this rent money and they would have these house-rent parties to raise their money. I got in with a bunch there, so I walked round dressed up in the day and played at night. It wasn't much, they give you a little something. Best you got was all you could drink, all you could eat and a good-looking woman to fan you, that's about the best you'd get."*

The statistics of the Depression are almost beyond belief. Unemployment rose from 3 million in 1930 to 11 million in 1932, then to as many as 15 million the following year. More than 5,500 banks and over 100,000 businesses had collapsed by 1932. A quarter of all the railroads were bankrupted. *'The gulf between rich and poor was so great that the 36,000 wealthiest families had incomes that equalled the total combined income of the 12 million poorest families. The living conditions of these families, or 42% of the population, barely reached the level of subsistence,'* was the estimate of one writer.

Whether in the devastated cities of the North and East or the rural wastelands of the South, black families endured privation on an unprecedented scale. The government of Herbert Hoover was not only unable to cope with the disaster, it was also unwilling, believing as it did in the all-American notion that recourse to public relief would undermine the individual's will for self-help.

The hundreds of store-front churches that had sprung up in city ghettoes in the 1920s were swamped by the needs of the community they served. Many set up 'thrift shops' selling clothes and shoes for a few cents. Some black churches were already highly organised, like the Olivet Baptist Church in Chicago which had a social welfare programme involving 42 departments with over 500 officers - 24 of them paid full-time, but even they were overwhelmed. Other religious figures, like the messianic Father Divine, traded public assistance for personal deification, establishing 'a massive co-operative, based on the biblical Last Supper' which provided meals free or very cheap and organised supplies of coal at cost. (Father Divine went on to become an influential figure in African-American politics, calling for *'a plan for a righteous government in which there will be equality for all mankind, with the abolition of such evils as lynching and Jim Crow practices.'*)

It would be difficult, if not impossible, to fully comprehend the initial significance of gospel music without appreciating the context of the Depression within which it took shape. Those early gospel songs were all set against this great tragedy. The antagonism with which they were received wasn't just because they had

Scenes from Thomas Dorsey's life. Top: with parents and family (Thomas is front left); Top right: Off to convention with friends. Below: At the grave of Mahalia Jackson (L); Teaching Mahalia at his home (R).

Photos: Author's Collection and Fisk University.

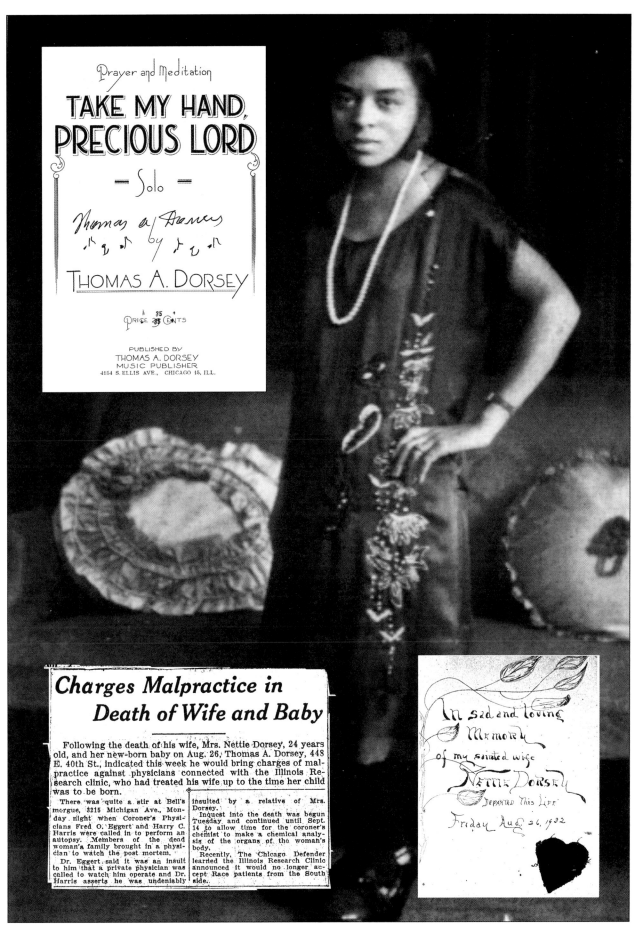

Mrs Nettie Dorsey. Insets: Thomas Dorsey responded to her death by writing gospel's masterwork. He also challenged the hospital over the tragedy; Nettie's epitaph in Thomas Dorsey's own hand (R).

the profane taint of the blues about them; it was also because they communicated an exceptional joy during a time of exceptional sorrow. Churches that were overcome with the poverty of a desperate flock were not in the mood for songs that they regarded not simply as secular but as frivolous.

In this sense, Dorsey was a truly prophetic figure in the church, affirming the central Christian theme of good news in a bad time. When he fixed you with a long bony finger and demanded to know, "*Down through the ages, gospel's what? What'd they say it was? You mean you don't know that ... good news?*", you can be sure that he wasn't just talking about a bunch of songs, however good they might be.

The Baptists succumbed first. The Jubilee Session of the National Baptist Convention was meeting in Chicago and Dorsey was there to drum up business. At least one of his songs had got there before him however and he was stunned to hear his own composition *If You See My Saviour* ringing round the huge Coliseum and *'laying them in the aisles'*. He promptly struck a bargain with the Convention's musical directors and began selling his music right there and then. Not all the Baptists were so easily persuaded but down at 4501 South Vincennes Ave, in the Ebenezer Baptist Church, Thomas Dorsey organised his first choir and established a base for the exhilarating new sound of gospel.

People came to Ebenezer from all over Chicago, and many more were getting to hear about this dynamic 33 year-old who was revolutionising church music. Sallie Martin was one who got to hear and she was down there like a shot, making her debut with Dorsey's little choir in February 1932. Dorsey ignored her completely at first, but Sallie wasn't the kind of person who'd take a back seat graciously and besides, she knew just how to handle bull-headed men from Georgia. She had been raised in Atlanta just like Dorsey, she'd made the same pilgrimage to Chicago for work and she'd not long since walked out on a boorish, drunken husband. Thomas A. was small fry for the combative Sallie and they quickly teamed up for what was to be an eight-year mission to spread the gospel of gospel music.

If Dorsey was the creative inspiration, Sallie Martin was the promotional genius. She was no great shakes as a singer's singer, she never could hit the sweet high notes nor could she seduce with the low, resonating moans of a gospel blues, but she knew that rare art of charging up an audience out of her own strength of conviction and very little else. "*Sallie can't sing a lick, but she can get over anywhere in the world,*" was Dorsey's pithy verdict. She performed as a great preacher performs, going out a little way in front of the audience then pausing, then articulating exactly what everyone else is on the point of articulating. Her way wasn't to impress by vocal skills but to catch hold of the spirit in a room and allow it to flood through her in a torrent of home truths and eternal wisdoms. It was something she'd brought with her from the Holiness churches and when it was harnessed to the vehicle of a Dorsey gospel song, there were very few listeners who were not anointed in that moment.

That same year they set about organising the very first National Convention of Gospel Choirs and Choruses (or the Gospel Singers Convention, to give it its original name). The two of them, together with Theodore Frye, were ambitious enough, shifting over to Dorsey's home church, the three-thousand-seater Pilgrim Baptist church. Come the day of the Convention however, South Indiana Avenue was solid with people trying to get in. The place was so packed that there was barely enough room for the chair. "*We had to put the director's stand halfway up the aisles, back of the church,*" Dorsey remembered with pleasure.

That first time, the young people just couldn't get enough gospel singing. The elders and the pastors weren't quite so sure about the merits or de-merits of this rocking, bluesy gospel but Thomas was quick to point out to them that putting a beat into a spiritual was only a way of bringing out what was there already: *"There's always been a beat as you call it in the church. If they didn't have a piano organ, they did it with their feet, pat their feet, pat their hands. There are moaning blues that are used in spirituals and there are moaning spirituals that are used in blues."* Privately he'd also continued to scorn the false divisions between sacred and secular. *"You know, the blues ain't nothing but a good woman feeling bad, while a good spiritual is something that lifts the heavy heart. Now tell me what's wrong about that?"*

The man who wrote the new gospel songs and the woman who first sang them, were beginning to sense that something momentous was taking shape. The Dorsey/Martin combination was starting to pack them in at Pilgrim and at Ebenezer Baptist Churches and people were eager to catch the new songs almost before the ink dried. With the city still in the depths of the Depression, the black church movement was growing daily as a focus and refuge for the dispossessed. People were hungry enough for food and clothing, but they were even hungrier for reasons to be hopeful. Governmental relief was one thing but no public body was supplying relief from spiritual poverty. Community programmes were saving people's lives but they weren't saving their souls. The churches weren't bulging at the seams because they were giving away soup and bread; they were filled with people starved of hope, strength, courage, dignity and happiness. The gospel music of Thomas Dorsey spoke directly to these needs in these circumstances, affording real comfort and affirming real joy. His revolution didn't lie in any kind of trivial musical rebellion but in creating a means whereby the poor could discover unfathomable riches. *"I wrote to give them something to lift them out of that depression. They could sing at church but the singing had no life, no spirit."*

> *Hide me in thy bosom till the storm of life is over,*
> *Rock me in the cradle of thy love.*
> *Feed me until I want no more,*
> *Then take me to my blessed home above.*

The classic Dorsey tunes were selling for 10 or 15 cents, but the recording industry had all but collapsed in the climate of austerity, with every big company taking its share of the common tragedy. The gospel movement, born as it was out of this social disaster, was running against the tide. Insofar as material suffering increased, so did the need and the demand for spiritual comfort and release - so gospel music boomed as society collapsed. The Dorsey songs directly reflected the experiences of the human condition in all its suffering and its triumphs, because they reflected his own sufferings and triumphs. His most perfect, most famous song *Precious Lord* is the best example ...

By the middle of the year, Thomas Dorsey could walk past any of the hundreds of store front churches and not be too surprised to hear one of his tunes filtering through the door. But this was just Chicago and both he and Sallie set out on the road to 'liven up' the churches in the other great cities, conducting revivals and setting up gospel choruses - the first in Cleveland, where Sallie was already known. Tragedy caught up with Thomas on the road though:

"I was in a revival and my wife was to become a mother and I was feeling that she'd make a lovely, lovely

mother when I got back. They said for me to come to the door of the hall where I received a telegram. I read it - I almost fell out. 'Hurry home. Your wife just died.' I don't know how you would accept that. I couldn't accept it at all. A friend of mine put me in the car and dropped me right home. When I got home I just ran in to see if it was true and someone goes 'Nettie just died, Nettie just died, Nettie just died.' The baby was still alive but within the next two days the baby died."

For a full week Dorsey was utterly stricken and inconsolable but he roused his spirits sufficiently to visit close friend Theodore Frye and pour out his anguish with some singing. *"Right there and then I began to sing, 'Precious Lord ... take my hand ... lead me on ... let me stand! ...' and I cast my burden on the Lord."*

Precious Lord is the most majestic of all the gospel anthems. There can be very few gospel singers who haven't at some point wrapped their vocal chords round the consummate beauty of its simple melody, who haven't revived a somnolent congregation with its lyrical supplication, who haven't been irresistibly compelled by the sheer economy of its themes, to take this song and make it their own. It's a masterpiece of gospel hymnody - part spiritual uplift, part blues melancholy - and it cries out to be sung with all the dramatic phrasing and curlicues that characterise the emotive gospel performance. It almost never fails to draw a response, even when sung by the most mediocre singer. In the hands of a front-rank gospel singer it assumes an awesome spiritual power. *"I don't know anyone that has written songs as heart-searching as Precious Lord. They come out of the experience in him, that's what he says. There's no sound that could equal Precious Lord; he wrote it when he was discouraged and his spirit was broken,"* said another of Dorsey's great pioneer singers, Willie Mae Ford Smith.

Amongst those pioneers, Sallie Martin was the first of a stream of young singers who took up with Dorsey in 1932. His proteges were many and, curiously, all were female - or at least all of those who came to any prominence. None have hinted that there might have been romantic attachments to Dorsey, though photographs taken at the time reveal him as a sharp dresser with a knowing smile and his past reputation as a risque songwriter would not have gone unnoticed. Perhaps it's simply a quirk of history that invites retrospective speculation but there's no doubt that the women singers were the first into the field with Thomas Dorsey's songs and that they all came to revere him as a father figure.

By the autumn of 1932, Dorsey and Sallie Martin were back on the road, taking the new songs to churches throughout the country. It was while they were down in St Louis, Missouri that they first met up with Willie Mae Ford Smith who became Dorsey disciple number two. Thomas summed her up in the typical manner of a bluesman. *"He said I had the vocal power to surpass Bessie Smith"*, remembered Willie Mae with some pride - like so many other young singers out of strict Baptist homes, she was a covert fan of the blues.

But, while surrounded by all the delights of blues and jazz, she remained solidly grounded in church music:

"My maternal grandmother, who had been a slave, used to baby-sit us while my mother worked. She used to amuse us by singing, clapping and doing the 'Rock Daniel', her name for the holy dance. She'd be in the spirit and we'd just copy her, playing like. I didn't shout until I was grown, when I had something to shout about."

The Chicago pioneers. Top: Theodore Frye (L), Roberta Martin (R). Below: Sallie Martin (L), Kenneth Morris (R)

Willie Mae came up the hard way. Originally from Rolling Fork, Mississippi, she was raised in Memphis along with her thirteen brothers and sisters. Father was a railway brakeman and a devout local deacon to whom singing came as natural as breathing. The kids slept four to a bed with their own coats as blankets but she didn't brood on the hardships. The memories that endured were of family love and homespun music. *"In 1922, I joined the family quartet, called the Ford Sisters, who were entertainers as well as evangelists. We were more like the spiritual version of the Mills Brothers!"* Two years later the Ford Sisters caused a minor sensation at the National Baptist Convention and a singing career became inevitable - though at that stage it might as easily have been in secular as sacred music. Even after meeting up with the Dorsey/Martin team and committing herself to organising St Louis for them, she still didn't consider her-self saved, and there was always as much chance of her singing for Cab Calloway as Thomas Dorsey.

The Church of God Apostolic finally took her in the late 1930s, but pentecostal fervour had always delin-eated her singing style and many a Baptist convention was thrown into serious commotion by Willie Mae's scorching solos. She worked in front of a congregation with the same emotional pitch of Sallie Martin, but unlike Sallie she was also a formidable vocalist in her own right. Even at the age of eighty and, like Dorsey and Martin, feted by an adoring new generation of gospel lovers, she still retained a vocal control and intensity of feeling that most singers half her age could never achieve. It's almost inconceivable that in all those years she was never recorded but, once committed to gospel, she sang only to evangelise and there were few personal considerations of career or reward. Willie Mae was one of those few who never sold out, never gave up and never made a thing out of gospel other than the satisfaction of working for her Saviour. *"My voice may crack as deep as the Mississippi River, but you know like the river, I just keep on rolling."* If anyone qualified as a bona fide gospel saint it was Willie Mae Ford Smith.

Back in 1932 though, she was just another child of the Depression, a church girl with a big voice and even bigger ideas, shaking up the Baptists as a Dorsey Disciple. She had that same blend of blues and sanctified and she got herself into the same kind of trouble for it: *"They said I was bringing the blues into the church"* she recalled in tones of real outrage, *"'You might as well be Mamie Smith, Bessie Smith, one of those Smith sis-ters, you make me sick with that stuff'. Well, I said, that's all the stuff I know. When I first started out singing gospel they said 'We don't want that coonshine stuff in here, we don't want that ragtime singing in here', but that didn't stop me. I kept going because that's what the Lord wanted."*

Willie Mae took on the job of organising the Soloists Bureau for Dorsey's National Convention of Gospel Choirs and Choruses and in so doing she inspired a whole string of young singers who all went on to become gospel legends - most of them gaining the kind of kudos that should have been hers. Up in Washington she fired up a young Edna Gallmon Cooke who later had successful albums with Nashboro Records; in Chicago it was Myrtle Scott, a reclusive figure who made legendary once-a-year appearances when she would sing just one song and completely wreck a church; in her home town of St Louis it was Martha Bass, who became a mainstay of the Ward Singers and a successful solo artist; Brother Joe May was her pupil too and gained considerable fame as 'The Thunderbolt of the Mid-West' with a straight (male) copy of her style. Mother Smith, as everyone affectionately came to know her, trained them all and inspired them all.

Someone else though was in the wings and getting inspiration from Willie Mae and Thomas Dorsey.

Someone who would become the greatest Dorsey protege of all and take gospel music to unimaginable heights. Someone who in that same year of 1932 was not far away, singing leads with Chicago's Greater Salem Baptist Church Choir and with its offshoot, the Johnson Gospel Singers.

Mahalia Jackson was twenty one and already a singer of extraordinary power. She'd come up to Chicago at sixteen, having absorbed all the music that her home town of New Orleans could offer. Hers was the most heavily blues-drenched background of any of the major gospel singers of the time and everyone who heard her said she could be Bessie Smith number two. She got offers of course - from big name jazzmen like Earl Hines, but she showed them all the door. Others would have been tempted, some would have wavered, still more would have capitulated, but there's not the slightest hint that Mahalia Jackson ever considered singing blues for a living. Not that she disapproved in any way - in fact she secretly played all the records just like Willie Mae.

> *"When did I first begin to sing?"* Mahalia Jackson had been asked the question by Studs Terkel, the Chicago journalist and critic. *"You might as well ask me when did I first begin to walk and talk. In New Orleans where I lived as a child, I remember singing as I scrubbed the floors. It would make the work go easier. When the old people weren't home, I'd turn on a Bessie Smith record. And play it over and over ... Bessie was my favourite, but I never let people know I listened to her. Mamie Smith has a prettier voice, but Bessie's had more soul in it. She dug right down and kept it in you. Her music haunted you even when she stopped singing."*

She spurned the blues for herself not because it was incompatible with her voice, but because it didn't suit her attitude to life. *"Blues are the songs of despair,"* she once said. *"Gospel songs are the songs of hope. When you sing gospel you have a feeling there's a cure for what's wrong. When you're through with the blues you've got nothing to rest on."*

The real musical inspirations of her girlhood in New Orleans probably lay outside of both the blues and her own Mount Moriah Baptist Church. In the latter case, literally outside it - the Holiness Church right next door, in that part of the city sandwiched between the river and the railway. Mahalia was endlessly fascinated with the Holiness manner of worship, with its echoes going all the way back to West Africa. *"These people had no choir or organ. They used the drum, the cymbal, the tambourine and the steel triangle. Everybody in there sang, and they clapped and stomped their feet, and sang with their whole bodies. They had a beat, a rhythm we held on to from slavery days, and their music was so strong and expressive. It used to bring tears to my eyes."* Whether through family ties or theological choice, Mahalia never converted to Holiness but she always favoured their style, even within the more decorous Baptist services:

> *"I loved best to sing in the congregation. All around me I could hear the foot-tapping and hand-clapping. That gave me the bounce. I liked it better than being up in the choir singing anthems. I liked to sing songs which testify to the glory of the Lord. Those anthems are too dead and cold for me. As David said in the Bible: 'Make a joyful noise unto the Lord.' That's me ... We Baptists sang sweet ... Where these Holiness people tore into I'm So Glad Jesus Lifted Me Up! they came out with real jubilation. I say: don't let the Devil steal the beat from the Lord! The Lord don't like us to act dead. If you feel it, tap your feet a little - dance to the glory of the Lord!"*

Mahalia Jackson took the Holiness fervour and she matched it with those old hymns of Dr Watts that were still so popular with black Baptists. *"Dr Watts?"* she exclaimed with delight, *"Now you're talking about the power. Those songs, hmmmm, they come out of conviction and suffering."* And though it's clear she was talking about the adoptive article rather than a London hymnwriter of comfortable means, she's nevertheless touching on the kind of universality that is in the work of any great spiritual songwriter - whether it be Isaac Watts in England or Thomas Dorsey in Chicago; *"The worst voices can get through singing them, 'cause they're telling their experiences."*

Chicago was alive with the new gospel sounds of Dorsey, of Sallie Martin and of Willie Mae Ford Smith. Willie Mae was an especial influence on the young Mahalia and encouraged her out of her little cosmetics business. *"She often told me, 'Willie Mae, I'm gonna leave this beauty shop, I wanna be like you' ... I liked her right off, she was more like me, a mover and a go-getter."* The raw southern sounds of Willie Mae's gospel singing so inspired Mahalia Jackson that she took all the various elements of the older woman's style and stirred it with her own into a potent brew of down-home singing. She wasn't above playing a little on the element of nostalgia either. *"Gospel music in those days of the early 1930s was really taking wing,"* she recalled in her book Movin' On Up. *"It was the kind of music colored people had left behind down South, and they liked it because it was just like a letter from home."*

The more sophisticated and middle class black Baptists in the northern cities weren't quite so taken with the idea of shouts and moans and Holiness excesses. It was all so retrogressive to them, a harking back to old indignities and ancient African roots they would rather consign to history. She tells the story of her 'one and only singing lesson' when Professor Dubois, a refined black tenor, tried to get her to adapt. *"You've got to learn to stop hollerin'. The way you sing is not a credit to the Negro race. You've got to learn to sing songs so that white people can understand them."* Even Thomas Dorsey, when later she partnered him as Sallie Martin's successor, tried in vain to polish her up a bit. *"I tried"*, he recalled with a wry smile, *"To show Mahalia how to breathe and phrase, but she wouldn't listen. She said I was trying to make a stereotyped singer out of her. She may have been right."*

By the middle of the 1930s, Mahalia was an established and popular solo singer, and on 21st May 1937 she cut her first recordings for the Decca-Coral label, with Estelle Allen accompanying her on piano and organ. She'd been married a year then, to a graduate of Fisk University, and the world must have seemed a very rosy place indeed for her; but neither the marriage nor the recording career lasted long. Her first record - *God's Gonna Separate The Wheat From The Tares* backed up with the old Baptist hymn *Keep Me Every Day* - is something of a gospel masterpiece and was a fair hit in the still depressed race market; but she didn't record again until more than ten years later. The intervening period was spent with Thomas Dorsey, who had parted company with Sallie Martin, and needed a replacement who could do his songs equal justice. Mahalia became his perfect musical foil and they travelled continuously together, raising the temperature at every church and programme they attended. Dorothy Love Coates of the Original Gospel Harmonettes remembers them at a convention in Birmingham, Alabama: *"It was amazing. Mr Dorsey would just keep handing Mahalia these ballads, and she'd stand there reading the words while she sang. She'd do fifteen, twenty songs a night like that."*

For many churches they raised the temperature higher than was proper and decent, for not only was

Mahalia Jackson at home in Chicago.

Mahalia an expressive soloist, she was also a flirtatious entertainer known for her 'snake-hips' and for lifting her robe an inch or two when she got happy. It's difficult to believe that the matronly figure who later came to personify gospel music at its most imperious, was once so outrageously sanctified in her performances that she'd get herself barred from respectable Baptist churches.

It didn't worry her, all this criticism from what she called those 'high-up society Negroes'. She was happiest anyway amongst those who had little to lose - the poor in everything but spirit who thronged the storefront churches to hear her magnificent contralto voice. She rocked them like a New Orleans ragtimer with Dorsey's *What Could I Do?* and she made them faint dead away with his *Precious Lord.* She roared and shouted like a pentecostal preacher, she moaned and growled like the old southern mothers, she hollered the gospel blues like a sanctified Bessie Smith and she cried into the Watts' hymns like she was back in a slave cabin. They say that, in her time, Mahalia Jackson could wreck a church in minutes flat and keep it that way for hours on end.

In 1946, Mahalia Jackson re-launched her recording career with four songs cut for Apollo in New York City on 3rd October. It was a first appearance for the young pianist Mildred Falls who became Mahalia's permanent accompanist for more than two decades. Mildred was there again the following year, together with organist Herbert Frances, for the second recording with Apollo. On 12th September, back in her Chicago stamping ground, Mahalia recorded a further four songs, one of which - W. H. Brewster's classic *Move On Up A Little Higher* - provided Mahalia with her (and gospel's) first million-selling record. Three months later she was back in the Chicago studios to make the sequel - *Dig A Little Deeper* - which sold over half-a-million copies.

Mahalia Jackson was gospel's first super-star, though at this stage she was still virtually unheard of outside the African-American churches and the 'race records' market. The transition from store-front Queen of Gospel to national matriarch, came in the early 1950s. A triumphant appearance at Carnegie Hall as soloist with the National Baptist Convention in 1950 was about as far as she could go within the confines of the church, and a wider audience beckoned when her Apollo recording of *I Can Put My Trust In Jesus* won a prestigious French award, leading to a first European tour. She sang in London in 1952 and Max Jones of the Melody Maker reviewed the Royal Albert Hall concert in glowing terms, adding *"...and she has charm, so that when she dances those little church steps at the end of a rocking number, you need a heart of stone to remain unsmiling."*

Back in America she began to be courted by the big white-owned media companies, who saw in her an opportunity for high earnings with little risk. By 1954 she had her own TV programme on Chicago's WBBM, which was part of the CBS network, and the same year she dropped Apollo after royalty disputes and signed to Columbia Records. It was a calculated business decision on Mahalia's part, that reflected a growing pre-occupation with things material - firstly as just recompense, later as a crude commercialism. John Hammond, the legendary A&R man for CBS (who later discovered and signed Aretha Franklin and Bob Dylan) told this story after her death:

> *"Mahalia was recording for Apollo Records and getting gypped, like all the artists. She called me in the early fifties to tell me that she had got an offer from Columbia. This was before I was working for*

Photos: Author's collection.

Rev Dr Martin Luther King Jr. Top: preaching in church.
Below (L), with Mahalia Jackson. Below (R), Mahalia Jackson at King's funeral.

Columbia. I told her 'Mahalia, if you want ads in Life, and to be known by the white audience, do it. But if you want to keep on singing for the black audience, forget signing with Columbia, because they don't know the black market at all.' She took up the offer from Columbia then ... and she lost the black market to a horrifying degree. I'd say that by her death she was playing to a 75 per cent white audience, maybe as high as 90 per cent. Columbia gave her the fancy accompaniments and the choirs, but the wonderful drive and looseness from the Apollo recordings was missing. Did Mahalia miss the black audience? Mahalia was only interested in money, to be specific with you."

This is an unfair assessment. Mahalia was weaned on poverty and raised on exploitation. She became one of the first gospel singers to apply business acumen as a line of first defence against the parasites who attached themselves to black religious music. Many are the gospel artists today who'll pay tribute to the shrewd good business sense they learnt from Mahalia Jackson. Shirley Caesar, current First Lady of Gospel, tells with delight the story of Mahalia arriving for a concert and listening as the promoter pleaded lack of funds to pay her. *"She'd put her hand to her throat and croak 'Halie's got a bad throat, I ain't sure I can sing' - that promoter soon found the money and her voice came back like magic!"* It's a naive and ultimately demeaning notion, to hold that a gospel artist should simply stand and sing the Lord's praises while leaving to others the distasteful business of calculating the profits. Mahalia had always been entrepreneurial - early on she'd had the beauty parlour and the florist's shop. Now she converted her reputation for southern cooking into a chain of *Mahalia Jackson Chicken Dinners* that, at one stage, rivalled Colonel Sanders. She used to say, *"He calls his finger-licking good ... I call mine tongue-licking good."* She was earning huge sums on the international concert circuit and she'd set up a string of property deals, generating an estate worth more than a million dollars at her death. Long before Berry Gordy, Mahalia Jackson was *the* great African-American success story.

But she was never a great one for extravagance or personal luxuries and she never wavered once from her gospel mission. Instead, her accumulated wealth enabled her to establish the *Mahalia Jackson Scholarship Foundation* and to become a loyal and active supporter of fellow Baptist, Dr Martin Luther King Jr. King adored Mahalia (saying hers was *'The greatest voice the world has ever known'*) who in turn pulled political strings for him in Mayor Daly's Chicago. She stood with him at the historic climax of the March on Washington in 1963 and sang *I Been 'Buked and I Been Scorned* to the quarter-million strong demonstration assembled below the Lincoln Memorial. On the day of his assassination, King had been planning the evening church service, specifically requesting his favourite hymn - Thomas Dorsey's *Precious Lord*. Fittingly, Mahalia travelled down to Atlanta for Martin Luther King's funeral on April 9th 1968 and, at the open air service in the grounds of Morehouse College, she distilled all the triumphs and tragedies of black America into an unbearably moving performance of *Precious Lord, Take My Hand*. It was the ultimate that gospel music could ever become - a work of the most profound hymnody conjoined to an awe-inspiring public witness during an iconic moment in African-American history. It was then impossible not to be touched by the sheer transcendence of it all.

One man who was with Martin Luther King planning that service on the day of the shooting was Rev W. Herbert Brewster - a sixty seven year old pioneer integrationist and a gospel hymnwriter described by Tony Heilbut as 'at the very least, a Milton to Thomas A. Dorsey's Shakespeare'. Brewster is indeed an enormously significant figure in the early development of gospel who was, in the early 1930s, doing much the same thing in Memphis as Dorsey was doing up in Chicago. He it was who wrote that first million-selling song for Mahalia Jackson - *Move On Up A Little Higher* (though for many years she claimed to have written it herself with Dorsey's old colleague Theodore Frye) and Mahalia recorded at least as many Brewster songs as Dorsey songs, including the classic *How I Got Over*. Brewster was magnanimous about Mahalia's copyright theft: *"They tried to get me to do something about it, but I said, I can't do that to Mahalia; if she wants it, let her take it, I can write a thousand."*

illiam Herbert Brewster, with Arts and Divinity degrees, arrived in Memphis as a young man from the rural Tennessee town of Summerville. His paternal grandfather was a slave preacher and he was raised on the poetry and eloquence of the old spirituals:

> *"The first spiritual that I heard was as a three year old in a log cabin in the middle of a cotton patch. In those days when I was born, the Black people lived close to the crops - right at the end of the cotton rows, right in your front yard among the most beautiful blooms. So one morning, everyone had gone to the fields after breakfast at four o'clock and my grandmother was the last to leave. I heard her singing and the room was filled with melody and music and it looked like the angels were singing or something. I got up and crept to the door. She was on the dirt floor of the kitchen that was built against that one room shanty, doing her chores. And she was singing a song. I shall never forget the words: 'I am a poor pilgrim of sorrow, left out in this world alone'. She was singing and laughing out loud almost hysterically - that 'Holy Ghost laugh' they used to call it. And then she would be crying. The tears were meeting under her chin. It touched my heart so deeply."*

East Trigg Baptist Church in Memphis became famous for the new music of its minister. Lyrically daring, as well as musically, Rev Brewster was known for his use of Christian metaphors to intimate the political advancement of black people. His 'move on up a little higher' wasn't simply a pietistic gesture heavenward, but a conscious statement about empowerment here on earth. In the heart of Tennessee in the wake of the Depression, that required exceptional courage.

> *"The fight for rights here in Memphis was pretty rough on the Black church. I was trying to inspire Black people to move up higher. Don't be satisfied with the mediocre. Move into the professions and move into politics. That was my doctrine. Before the freedom fights started, before the Martin Luther King days, I had to lead a lot of protest meetings. In order to get my message over, there were things that were almost dangerous to say, but you could sing it."*

His great singing disciple was named after Queen Candice of Ethiopia, and joined East Trigg Choir in the late 30s. Within a few years, Queen C. Anderson became a renowned gospel name throughout the South and, though her voice never really transferred to record, she drew huge crowds to her enthralling performances of Brewster's songs. In many ways, Brewster rivalled Dorsey as a gospel songwriter, blending a rich and hopeful biblical imagery with a succession of timeless melodies. Above all, his songs combined literary insight with folk wisdom. *"A good gospel song"* he said, *"Is a sermon set to music. It must have sentiment and doctrine, rhetorical beauty and splendour."* It's evident even in the titles of his classic songs, still in common currency today: *Treading The Wine Press Alone, How Far Am I From Canaan* (*"...the boy from the Soul Stirrers, Sam Cooke, made that popular. He came here and I taught it to him"*), *Weeping May Endure For A*

Top: Rev Brewster preaching at Sunday service, East Trigg Baptist Church, Memphis.
Below: Rev W. Herbert Brewster (L); Queen C. Anderson (R).

Photos: East Trigg Baptist Church.

Night, These Are They, My Soul Looks Back And Wonders How I Got Over and *Surely God Is Able.*

Brewster's genius is only recently receiving due recognition, while others have made their names and their fortunes with his songs. He remained at East Trigg throughout his life, becoming a political figure almost as much as a religious leader in Memphis. During the 1950s his reputation, and that of Queen C. Anderson, was such that the young Elvis Presley would regularly show up for Sunday services at East Trigg, absorbing the gospel music he later combined with blues and country music to launch white rock 'n roll. There were no Brewster songs amongst the Presley big sellers and royalties aren't payable on inspiration, but Presley did sell a million copies of another classic gospel song - Thomas Dorsey's *Peace In The Valley.*

ospel publishing, as distinct from recording, was in its infancy when Dorsey began to issue his songs in 1932. Sallie Martin spotted the opportunity first on her initial trip to Cleveland in 1933, when she sold some of Dorsey's sheet music for ten dollars:

> *"People would come into Mr Dorsey's home to buy music, and so one day after they had finished, he was living with his uncle you see, he had a sack in his drawer in which he'd keep his money, and if his niece wanted to go to the store, she'd just go and get the money out, and never say how much out and how much in and I noticed that. I said 'You have something here but you don't know what to do with it'."*

Dorsey didn't always take to Sallie's abrasive and inquisitive ways but he recognised her organisational skills *"You think you could do better?"* he asked, drawing an emphatic response from Sallie. They struck a deal and he paid her the grand sum of four dollars a week.

By the time Sallie Martin split up with Dorsey in 1940, through petty misunderstandings and personality clashes, gospel music sales were once again in full flood. The collapse of the 'race' records market during the Depression had been all but complete. During the years of 1932 and 1933, the number of spiritual records was cut back even more drastically than blues. Bluebird Records did an isolated recording of the eternally popular Rev Gates in 1934 but not again for the next five years. Rev J. C. Burnett cut six titles near the end of the 1930s but the boom in sermon records (over 300 were issued in five years up until 1931, most of them by Rev Gates) had come to an end. Insofar as there was any great recording activity in the 1930s, it fell mainly to the jubilee quartets, and even then much of it was re-issues of earlier sessions.

Discographers Dixon and Godrich have found that, *'In 1934 there had been only eight quartet records, but the number gradually built up until in 1938 there were over fifty, the level of the peak years. Every label had its regular quartet - Mitchell's Christian Singers on Vocalion, the Heavenly Gospel Singers on Bluebird, and Paramount's Norfolk Jubilee Quartet on Decca.'* The guitar evangelists fared little better. Joshua White did some sacred recordings in 1934 and Decca brought back Blind Joe Taggart the same year. The following year they added a few spiritual songs from Blind Willie McTell but interest was fading fast.

In 1938, not one single new recording was issued, but a year later the market had recovered to the extent that sacred records formed a quarter of all 'race' releases. Once again it was Rev Gates, with increasingly outrageous sermons like *Will Hell Be Your Santa Claus?* and *Smoking Woman On The Street* recorded for

Victor in 1939. The Golden Gate Jubilee Quartet (see next chapter) were also extremely popular - with their acapella close harmony entertainment based on spirituals. Between 1920 and 1942, about 1,250 spiritual and gospel records were issued.

Almost none of this mass of recording activity reflected the activities of the Dorsey pioneers. Gospel music proper was a radical departure in the middle of a Depression. It would have represented a commercial risk to the companies at the best of times. In the 1930s it was beyond even elementary consideration as a sales prospect. Whatever small budget there was for recording got spent on the safe bets - the big name preachers and the jubilee quartets - and the rest of the catalogues were padded out with old recordings, sometimes put out under different artists' names and often issued many times on different labels. The commercial business therefore for the new generation of gospel artists lay, not so much in recording, but in song publishing.

Having left Dorsey, Sallie Martin gravitated to the First Church of Deliverance on Chicago's South Wabash Avenue, where the extrovert Rev Clarence Cobb presided over a Spiritualist congregation. Cobb wasted little time in setting her up with pianist and songwriter Kenneth Morris, and together they founded the *Martin and Morris Publishing Company*. Their first hit was with an arrangement of *Just A Closer Walk With Thee* and it was Kenneth Morris who later wrote *Dig A Little Deeper*, which sold half-a-million copies for Mahalia Jackson in 1947. Until 1945, however, there was still no recording of the new gospel music and sheet-music was the only outlet, garnering sales in the hundreds of thousands. At ten or fifteen cents a time, that began to add up in a big way.

Roberta Martin was unrelated to Sallie, but she was yet another ardent Dorsey disciple of the early 1930s, emerging from his first choir at Ebenezer Baptist Church. Her career isn't so well documented as Mahalia's, but she grew in stature and reputation until she rivalled Queen Mahalia in the people's affections. Roberta and Sallie teamed up briefly, using some of the best young male singers - Robert Anderson, Eugene Smith, Norsalus McKissick and Willie Webb - to form the Martin and Martin Gospel Singers. The liaison of namesakes was short-lived, neither woman ready to risk being in the shadow of the other, and Roberta took the group on to international fame.

The retitled Roberta Martin Singers presaged all the other thousands upon thousands of gospel groups that followed. Roberta became, like Sallie, a powerful publisher of gospel through her own Martin Studio of Gospel Music and Roberta Martin came to personify gospel music every bit as much as Mahalia. The people of Chicago especially idolised her - when she died in 1969, more than 50,000 passed through Mount Pisgah Baptist Church to view her body and pay their last respects to a gospel madonna.

Sallie Martin, meanwhile, had formed her own group of singers - one of the first ever all-female groups in gospel. The Original Sallie Martin Singers' line-up, in a 1940 photograph taken at a Virginia revival, shows Sallie with a very young Ruth Jones (who later changed her name to Dinah Washington and became the mother of rhythm and blues), Necie Morris (Kenneth's wife) and Sarah Daniels. The personnel changed frequently and early on, Sallie brought in her adopted daughter Cora as soloist.

The Chicago pioneers extended the orbit of gospel music over the next few years, travelling to programmes thousands of miles apart, even as far as Los Angeles, which had yet to encounter the new music. Eugene Smith of the Roberta Martin Singers recalled the epic tours:

"We used to leave Chicago right after New Year's. We had many, many engagements that started New Year's Eve night. We didn't get back to Chicago until June! In the winter we would go to California or Florida. We would work from Jacksonville all the way down to Key West. By the time we would come out of Florida, the weather would be nice in this area, and we would go into Philadelphia, where for a number of years we sang at Mount Carmel Baptist Church from Palm Sunday to Easter Sunday, over thirty years."

Another of the Roberta Martin Singers, Archie Dennis, explained their motivation on the road:

"We were committed to a ministry; dollars and cents had nothing to do with it. We rode for hundreds of miles in cars, had money in our pockets, but we couldn't go in the restaurants, so we went in grocery stores. We'd buy a loaf of bread and some baloney and some Miracle Whip and get an ice-cream stick to spread it on the bread. It was like a marriage. We had no other alternative, because the message was greater than we are. Any way the thing went, we were committed to it, the lean weeks and the weeks when we got above what we expected. One of the things Miss Martin taught us was a style of living. She taught us that God will endeavour to make the song and the singer one, and that you could sing a lie as well as tell one. At the time I was the youngest member of the group. They taught me and loved me and showed me that it's not just a song, but it's a life to be lived."

The early Chicago veterans built the gospel highway and in so doing they enshrined their home base forever as the fount of great gospel music. Thomas Dorsey, Sallie Martin, Mahalia Jackson, Roberta Martin, Willie Mae Ford Smith and Kenneth Morris, started out on a momentous journey in the 1930s. Evangelists all, they went in search of America's soul.

These weren't simply singers and songwriters concerned with making a way for themselves; they were quite literally ministers of the Christian gospel, communicators of good news through a new medium of song. In some ways, the excellence of their art makes it easy to forget that we're talking about a liturgical phenomenon as much as (if not more than) a musical one. The tradition of African-American worship as it evolved from slave songs and spirituals, was making a quantum leap here which would set it once again centre-stage in an increasingly secular drama. The Chicago pioneers set out to save souls but ultimately their achievement was to rescue urban culture from despair.

Nothing that followed in African-American music and very little that happened in Western popular music generally, would remain untouched in some way by this new sound they called gospel. ❖

Photo: Author's collection.

The Happyland Jubilee Singers c.1940, later to become the Five Blind Boys of Alabama.

Rev Claude Jeter of the Swan Silvertones, greets friends in New York.

Photo: Val Wilmer.

MOVING UP THE KING'S HIGHWAY

The Golden Age of Gospel Music

The Second World War marked the watershed of gospel music and ushered in its golden age. Between 1945 and 1965, countless thousands of gospel groups formed, toured, recorded and disbanded. Every town, every city, every county with a sizeable African-American community could boast a few quartets or gospel singers who mostly sang for free-will offerings at local church programmes and took the odd chance to make a few records. Immediately following the War, dozens of independent record companies were set up to serve the renewed demand for gospel, offering performers a chance of wider exposure but very little else. The standard agreement being around $50 per selection and the slimmest possibility of royalties.

With so many superb groups emerging and eager to record, few escaped the double-dealing and exploitation unless, like the legendary Kings of Harmony who originated from Alabama to become one of the finest of gospel quartets, they avoided record companies altogether. Fortunately for us, even groups such as they, were occasionally enticed into a studio for perhaps only two or three songs, leaving us with just a taste of their music. The Kings' one session in 1946 included Dorsey's *Precious Lord* and *God Shall Wipe All Tears Away*, hinting at a vocal imperative which was said to induce religious convulsions amongst their audiences. House-wrecking they called it.

The hard men of gospel quartet, the house-wreckers who took the older style of jubilee quartet and set its meticulous harmonies against a roaring lead voice, had been gathering their forces throughout the pre-war years. Independently of Dorsey and the Chicago pioneers, quartets - almost exclusively male - had been developing out of two main regional sources. The fount of quartet in the South was the area of Jefferson County in Alabama (specifically the towns of Birmingham, Bessemer and Fairfield) and traceable largely to the work of one man - R. C. Foster. Foster had arrived in Jefferson County in 1915, schooled in the art of university quartet singing by a Tuskagee Institute graduate, Professor Vernon Barnett. This of course was the measured, even way of spiritual singing we know from the Fisk Jubilee Singers - *".. when it come down, it come down just like one solid voice and it sound just like a brass band! And that's what the white folks said, 'I can't understand how you manage to do that?' Well me neither! I can't explain it."* The original Foster Singers never recorded but they primed the whole area for magnificent quartets like the Birmingham Jubilee Singers formed by the ubiquitous Charles Bridges in 1925 and Silas Steele's Famous Blue Jay Singers, formed a year later. The Blue Jays, along with the Kings of Harmony, are often cited as progenitors of the hard gospel quartet style and by 1930, the entire county was blessed with groups of unprecedented power and quality - the Heavenly Gospel Singers, the Four Great Wonders, the Fairfield Four, the Dunham Jubilee Singers, the Sterling Jubilees of Bessemer and the Ravizee Singers.

Out of Jefferson County, the groups began touring on a hand-to-mouth basis, spreading the word. Rev Isaac Ravizee recalled for Doug Seroff his first out-of-town trip:

> *"One of our first trips was in Mississippi. Laurel, Hattiesburg, Picayune, Amory, Jackson, Mississippi. We went from there to Vicksburg and we left Vicksburg going to Monroe, Louisiana. Where we really got stranded was in a little old place called Bass Trap, Louisiana. There was a Baptist State Convention going on there and it was largely attended. There were some people from Mobile there, one of the ladies was Daisy Fisher. When she saw us on the yard she said 'Oh, here are the Ravizee Singers!' She went in and contacted the president of the State Convention and made a request to allow the Ravizees to sing. When we sung, we were stranded. We really didn't have any money and the car was broken down. When we got through singing they took up a collection of about $170. After we sang, the people were shouting and they heard it across the street at the church where the Women's Auxiliary of the Convention was meeting and they wanted to hear the Ravizee Singers too. So we went over there and it was almost pandemonium over there. They wanted to know how much the men raised and someone told them and they said 'We're going to beat them.' And they gave us $200."*

Thus the groups, and the Alabama innovations in quartet singing, travelled the country.

While the Jefferson County singers fanned out across the South and Mid-West, the other great source of gospel quartet was serving the East Coast. For some curious reason, the Tidewater region of Virginia was the birthplace of numerous fine male quartets which by 1923 included the innovative Norfolk Jubilee Quartet (who also recorded as the Norfolk Jazz Quartet) as well as the Silver Leaf Quartette, the Excelsior Quartet, the Pearly Gates of Suffolk and many others. Like the Jefferson County groups, a direct line can be traced from the Tidewater groups back to the university quartet tradition - in this case the

Photos: Viv Broughton/Ray Funk.

Top: The current lineup of the Fairfield Four (L), and as they were in 1947.
Below: The Golden Gate Quartet.

local Hampton Institute Quartet - and indeed, the traditions were largely maintained. Tidewater's church-es were known to be stiff and conservative, vigorously opposed to syncopation and any form of exhibition-ism. Since they provided the venues, they also called the tune but one group at least managed to break out and became the most widely copied and successful of all the gospel quartets - the Golden Gate Quartet.

The Golden Gates are generally credited as being the first to introduce the rhythmic spiritual and there are certainly no recordings in this style before 1936, when they cut their first sides for Bluebird Records. Again it's a Dorsey song that features, with Henry Owens, William Langford, Willie Johnson and Orlandus Wilson contributing perhaps the earliest known version of *Standing By The Bedside of A Neighbour*. In later years they clowned their way to show business prominence, moving even-tually to France where they still sing today, but in their time they were both entertaining and revolution-ary. Just before his death from cancer in 1980, founder member Willie Johnson was interviewed by Doug Seroff, and recalled the formation of the Golden Gates:

> *"We used to get together in Eddie Griffin's barbershop. At that time we weren't singing the type of stuff*
> *that we sang later. We were singing the run-of-the-mill things, like the old Fisk songs. The slow beat songs*
> *... we were singing in every church that let a quartet sing in it. And particularly, the main churches that*
> *got to me were the Holiness Churches, because they sang with a beat. And whenever I got around to*
> *training the group, I'd give our things a beat, upbeat it you know. That, in some churches the preachers*
> *wouldn't allow you to do! That was sinful stuff! You was singing the Lord's song with a beat and that was*
> *like dancing! So we overcame that ... I think with this quartet what we tried to create was what I used to*
> *call 'vocal percussion'. It was just like a drum but it had notes to it, it had lyrics to it you see. And you*
> *had different beats, you had different accents. Like a bunch of guys beating a tom-tom somewhere, and*
> *that's what it had to sound like. It all had to be done sharply and together, along with the harmony, and*
> *we sang simple chords. We were trying to sing chords that sounded good to the ear."*

The Golden Gates were Tidewater's ambassador group, pioneering the new forms of male gospel quartet at the same time as the Chicago team around Thomas Dorsey was starting out. Chicago too had direct links with the quartet tradition from the Southern regional source of Jefferson County. Norman McQueen, who had sung lead in the original Foster Singers of Bessemer, had moved up to Chicago and formed the *Chicago Progressive Quartet Association* in March 1931 with the motto 'Do all the good we can in all the places we can find'. The Association of more than twenty-five local quartets was active during the 1930s, opening up the airwaves for the first live broadcasting of gospel quartet and organising benefit programmes during the Depression years.

By the 1940s, many hundreds of black gospel quartets were on the road as full-time professionals and many thousands more worked as week-enders. Singing nearly always *a capella* (without instruments) it was the era of greatest artistic importance for gospel's male vocalists, producing such works of the human voice as were never heard before and have rarely been heard since. A great deal of the music was cap-tured on record but much of the history of the groups themselves is tragically missing.

Ironically, the period of gospel's most fertile activity is also the most hidden and it's only in recent years

Photos: Roy Francis/Ray Funk.

Ira Tucker and (inset) the Dixie Hummingbirds.

that a picture has begun to emerge through the dedication of a handful of researchers, collectors and historians who are painstakingly tracking down surviving group members and interviewing them in depth. It warrants - and one day will hopefully get - a three-volume history all to itself. However, it does seem from their research, that very few gospel groups who recorded before the Second World War also continued to record after it. It was a whole new ball-game for the great quartets who dominated gospel music over the next decade or so; the only real exception being the magnificent Dixie Hummingbirds, organised by James B. Davis in the mid-1930s, who managed to cut sixteen sides for Decca just as the war broke out. Even though they scored a regional hit with *Joshua Journeyed To Jericho*, it was five years before they recorded again - this time for Regis-Manor - by which point they'd picked up long-termers Willie Bobo from out of the Heavenly Gospel Singers and the legendary hard lead voice of Ira Tucker. Both Apollo and Gotham recorded them (twice in collaboration with the all-female Angelic Gospel Singers) until they finally settled with Don Robey's Peacock label in 1952, where they consolidated their formidable reputation.

The Hummingbirds - and Ira Tucker especially - remained at the head of gospel quartet for almost forty years, becoming the grand masters of the style. Always versatile and progressive in their harmonies, they could also pile on the emotional pressure and slay an audience in the Spirit ... once literally; at a Sunday concert in Ohio a woman collapsed and died from the intensity generated by Tucker as he sang *I'm Still Living On Mother's Prayer*. They toned it down a little after that but retained a distinctive urgency which they combined with more than a dash of showmanship. It was they who introduced the hip-slapping that male quartets became famous for, and they took audience involvement to new extremes way back in 1944 when Tucker first broke out from the stationary posture of male leads and leapt off the stage: *"I was singing I Don't Know Why by Thomas A. Dorsey and the folks had fits!"*

Later years saw them in the role of elder statesmen - still employing lush, progressive harmonies and abrasive leads but also indulging the huge crowds with wicked impersonations of younger rivals - a feature they called 'Let's Go Out To The Programs'. In 1966, the Dixie Hummingbirds took the Newport Jazz Festival by storm and they seemed set for widespread popular acclaim but, despite occasional guest spots with Paul Simon, their harmonic innovations became the stuff of legend and reference only.

It would appear to be the cross that all of the great quartets must bear. The Swan Silvertones and the Spirit of Memphis go back almost as far as the Hummingbirds and both created a vocal music which holds up even today for both spiritual drama and awe-inspiring technique. The former quartet were organised by the Alabama born master of falsetto singing, Claude Jeter, out of the Four Harmony Kings. Jeter and his brother had relocated to West Virginia and formed the group in 1938. Fearing confusion with the original Kings of Harmony, they switched names and became the Silvertone Singers. A weekly broadcast over WBIR in Knoxville, Tennessee captivated the local Swan Brothers Bakery, who became the group's sponsor over the next five years and bestowed on them the Swan prefix.

"There were only a few stations across the country playing gospel on the air so it was rough," Jeter remembers. *"It was just like nothin'. People had to put out handbills, posters, go through the city with a sound truck. That's how we had to make it. We were cutting down hedges and pavin' the way for singers today. Once in Pulaski, Virginia, we got ready to leave and we had 20 cents between all four of us! A ticket to a church program was 15 cents for children, 20 cents for adults. The sponsoring church or auxil-*

iary in the church would take 50 per cent of the house money, say $40, which left the four of us with $20. By the time we'd fill up the car, pay expenses (we'd pay $1 each to stay overnight someplace) we weren't making anything. It's something I wouldn't want to go through anymore, but we survived. We were born into singing gospel - if it hadn't been a part of us, we wouldn't have stayed out there and done it. We would have quit and got a job."

Hundreds of radio hours spent around a single microphone honed the group to unusual smoothness, which they later contrasted (not altogether willingly) with a succession of hard-driving leads - first **Solomon Womack** who recorded with them for King Records in the late 1940s and early 1950s, joined by the amazing **Robert Crenshaw** who screamed ecstatically all over their early Speciality recordings. Most of their unencumbered vocal music remains unmatched for subtlety, tension and dramatic counterpoint. That it also imposes its intentions on the human soul with such deft artistry, is nothing less than miraculous. Claude Jeter and the Swan Silvertones created a religious music equal to the finest in any other field and their best recordings - *Saviour Pass Me Not, Jesus Remembers, My Rock* - should be recognised as masterpieces.

In the mid-1960s, Claude Jeter quit the Swan Silvertones and became an ordained minister of the Church of Holiness Science in Detroit, later to retire to a modest brownstone apartment in New York. The tall, skinny genius of falsetto gospel reflected then that...

"... this is a thing where you can only survive by being real. Out of all the people we can fool, we can't fool God. He knows our intentions. So I'd rather fool nobody in the gospel field. If I don't feel the spirit, I won't move. I believe in the soft approach. The Bible tells us, 'If you pray in secret, I'll reward you openly.' I tried to practice that during my career."

The Spirit of Memphis go back even further than the Silvertones - some reports suggest as early as 1928 with original members **Arthur Wright, Luther McGill, James Peoples** and **James Darling**. They were re-organised a few years later, taking their name from Lindberg's plane, the Spirit of St Louis. One of their longest serving members was **Earl Malone**, who joined the group out of their junior section when he was 18 and was still singing with them almost sixty years later! Yet even he could remember a time when he was looking up to them from the sidelines. *"I was a small lad at that time when it got started,"* he said. *"And they used to walk everywhere they'd go. They used to walk up and down the street singing, and I used to sit in my porch and see them going by. And that's all that was in my mind, to one day be a member of the Spirit of Memphis."*

Through the 30s the group stuck mostly to the local area, keeping up their day jobs - Malone worked at the National Biscuit Company - and singing on weekends. Not until they were well into their second decade did the group begin travelling outside of Tennessee. *"It was just before we made our first recording,"* Malone recalled. *"Silas Steele had joined us. He was a member of the Blue Jays - they were already famous - and they were in town and heard us. He was impressed. He said 'Y'all are good enough to go on the road.' So he joined us, and we started riding trains."* Leaving their jobs, they took on another phenomenal lead voice in the form of **Jethroe Bledsoe** and set off on their professional career in the autumn of 1949. *"We went to Birmingham, and there was a fellow down there, and he made a cut on us. The record didn't really go anywhere,*

The Spirit of Memphis in 1984. L-R (rear) Melvin Mosley, Clifford Jackson, Robert Reed, Jimmie Allen, Earl Malone; (front) Jack Stepter, Brown Berry, Hubert Crawford. Inset: As they were in the mid 30s.

Photos: Lawrence Jasud/ Ray Funk.

but he made some money on it. But then Deluxe Records came in and bought the rights to the master from him, and then King took over, King bought De Luxe out." The much dealt-over first recordings were in fact issued under the name **Memphis Gospel Singers** and comprised just two tracks - *Happy In The Service of The Lord* and *My Life In His Hands*.

It was the beginning of an illustrious recording career for the **Spirit of Memphis** - their work for King and later **Peacock Records** having a peerless quality, especially with **Wilbur 'Little Axe' Broadnax** joining **Steele** and **Bledsoe** in a triumvirate of leads. Their trademark was their subdued emotional intensity.

"Our first trip to Chicago, the Soul Stirrers brought us up there as a favour because we'd brought them to Memphis. The people up there, they couldn't believe it. They thought we were the greatest thing that'd ever been up there. Because we didn't sing real loud at all, we just sung a bit above a whisper. We were all harmony - we didn't go for all the hollering."

The **Spirit of Memphis**, like the **Swan Silvertones**, were on the road for a good twenty five years and they're still active even now, though only **Earl Malone** and **Robert Reed** survive from the early line-up. Over the years they included **O. V. Wright** and **Joe Hinton** who both got taken into **R&B** by the boss of **Peacock Records** and **Brother Theo Wade** who later moved into radio with **WDIA** until his death in 1980. The great **Silas Steele** had a stroke on stage and died in **California**:

"Now he was the sort of guy, you just didn't know what he'd do next. When he sang at our concerts and you might say the house had been demolished, with all the people going out the door at the end of the night, he'd just stop them right in their tracks. And he could re-open the house again ... never did give up. If he felt there was something left to do he'd do it!"

When they celebrated their fiftieth anniversary at **Mason's Temple** in **Memphis**, **Earl Malone** reflected on a lifetime in spiritual music, *"The people who've come to Christ after hearing us sing. I think that's the best part of what we've done."*

At the other end of the post-war quartet spectrum stood the **Sensational Nightingales** and another legend - **Rev Julius Cheeks**. Where the **Silvertones** and the **Spirit of Memphis** captivated audiences with exquisite understatements, the **Sensational Nightingales** devastated them with diamond hard harmony and the primeval roaring lead of **Julius 'June' Cheeks**. **Jo Jo Wallace**, who sang tenor with the **Nightingales** for thirty years, was brought up on the softer jubilee stylings of the **Golden Gates** and the **Jubalaires** and remembers the shock of joining the **Nightingales**:

"It was almost like pulling my insides out, trying to sing behind Cheeks. I'd be hoarse every night. I nearly killed myself trying to make it with the Nightingales! I wasn't used to that style."

Julius Cheeks was born into grinding poverty in the same South Carolina town **Ira Tucker** comes from. *"It were bad, man. We didn't have a clock, we told time by the sun. We didn't eat right, we lived off fat-back and molasses. All us kids worked in the cotton fields, and Mama would whip me every day ... but she kept us straight."* No proper schooling meant that he couldn't read or write, but he got himself a recorded Bible

Top: Clarence Fountain and the Alabama Blind Boys. Below: Rev Julius Cheeks of the
Sensational Nightingales. Inset: Quartet 'Battles' were regular crowd pullers.

Photo of Julius Cheeks by
kind permission of Judy Cheeks.

when he was twenty-four and played it to death. His first singing group was the Baronets, who managed to impress the Nightingales when they passed through for a programme. The next day they came and collected him from the filling station where he worked and began training him.

"Our manager made us get up at eight or nine and we'd rehearse till lunchtime. Man, it was like gettin' out there plowin'. We'd hang a broom from the ceiling like a mike, and we sang all around it. After lunch, we'd get right back into rehearsal."

The Nightingales made their first recordings in the same year as the Spirit of Memphis - 1949. They went on to record for both King and Decca but their best material is preserved on the Peacock recordings of the mid-1950s with songs like *Standing In The Judgement, The Blood of Jesus, It Is No Secret* and *Burying Ground.* They're classic hard quartet tracks and essential in any gospel collection - stirring songs performed at the outer limits of vocal harmony. Carl Coates of the Nightingales, leaning on the porch of the modest Birmingham home he retired to with his wife Dorothy Love, recalled how long it took to cut the albums these songs were part of: *"Three, four hours man. That's all. Don Robey had us rehearse up, then in we'd go; one or two takes at most."*

Julius 'June' Cheeks died in 1980, having left instructions that his body not be taken further South than the Fourteenth Street Bridge in Baltimore, signifying his fierce hatred of southern racism. His voice was lacerated from his twelve years on the road with the Nightingales and some say he just about sang himself to death, impervious to the warnings of doctors, until his voice - never a refined instrument at the best of times - began to sound like gravel in a tin bucket. His was the rawest of gospel's baritones - moving and painful in its evocation of the roughest side of the mountain. Listening to the Nightingales, it's possible to understand that Cheeks wasn't simply indulging in nostalgia when he said towards the end of his life, *"I sit home sometimes and play my old records. I just cry. It'll make you cry, you know."*

Archie Brownlee died early too. At 2 o'clock on 8th February 1960, the hardest quartet singer of all time gave way to pneumonia in the New Orleans Charity Hospital. He was Cheeks' big rival on the circuit, the inheritor of Silas Steele's mantle as the star voice of quartet. One old time singer recalled, *"My style wasn't broken until Archie Brownlee, he come in ... I mean, I seen him at Booker T. Auditorium jump all the way off that balcony, down on the floor - blind! I don't see how in the world he could do that. People would just fall out all over the house!"*

Brownlee was the high-pitched screaming lead singer of the Five Blind Boys of Mississippi and they had a formidable reputation as a live gospel act. So much so that for a while in New Orleans they were required by the mayor to put up a Peace Bond because they were sending so many members of the congregation to hospital. The spirit ran so high when the Blind Boys hit a church that people went into comas - those who didn't come out of it were ferried off in ambulances.

The Five Blind Boys came out of the Piney Woods School for the blind, near Jackson, Mississippi, where they had learned to sing spirituals while still young boys. The Principal of the school, Lawrence Jones, had been organising fund-raising quartets as early as 1922 which all went under the name of Cotton Blossom Singers. Archie Brownlee, Lloyd Woodard, Isaiah Patterson, Joseph Ford and Lawrence Abrams were just

*Archie Brownlee and the classic 50s line-up
of the Five Blind Boys of Mississippi.*

Photo: Author's collection.

kids when they set out in the early 40s to do their bit for the School's funds, touring as the Cotton Blossom Singers for several months at a time and singing to audiences of wealthy white benefactors. Leaving the school in 1944, they began a professional career as the Jackson Harmoneers, travelling first up to Chicago and to programmes all over the South. By the time they cut their first records for Excelsior in 1946, they'd been joined by Rev Percell Perkins, an experienced lead singer who'd worked with groups like the Fairfield Four and the Soprocco Singers. Perkins took them over as manager and is fond of telling how he shaped their style from steady spirituals to the hard driving quartet they were later famous as. Now with their nickname formalised, the Five Blind Boys recorded ten songs for Coleman in New Jersey before signing a five year contract with the shady boss of Peacock Records, Don Robey. They were Robey's very first gospel group in 1950 and he was so impressed with their record sales that he moved on to sign up the biggest roster of gospel groups in the golden era.

Archie Brownlee and the Five Blind Boys began to hit big, moving out of the church programmes and packing auditoriums with anything up to 40,000 people - the Cow Palace in Dallas, the Keil Auditorium in St Louis, Convention Hall in Los Angeles and the Golden Gate Auditorium. One time in Dallas, Rev Perkins recalled that the Blind Boys got paid as much as $5,000 for one night's appearance, but that was exceptional and mostly their tale is a familiar one of big crowds, small fees and regular short-changing by tricky promoters. The music took them through it all, some of the most electrifying in all gospel and a great deal of it was captured on record. Even after Brownlee's incredible falsetto screams had been finally silenced and the personnel had altered dramatically, the Five Blind Boys continued to make intense, committed records. When they made their only visit to Europe in the mid-1960s, they displayed a rare Christian fervour and proved that in Rev Willie Mincy and Henry Johnson they still had lead singers who could rattle the windows of Hell.

By a complete coincidence, a second gospel quartet emerged around the same time, from the Talladega Institute for the Deaf and Blind over in Alabama. The Original Five Blind Boys of Alabama were formed by the late Velma Traylor, who was killed in a road accident in Blowing Springs, Georgia in 1947. A year later, the original line-up of lead singer Clarence Fountain, Olice Thomas, Johnny Fields and George Scott had been joined by Rev Paul Exkano, minister of the King Soloman Baptist Church in New Orleans and a member of that city's Chosen Five quartet. Paul Exkano shared the group's management duties with bass-man Johnny Fields - an outstanding student at the Blind School who had majored in business administration - and guided them to their first recording session for Coleman. Like the Mississippi Blind Boys they often went under a different name - in their case they were also known as the Happyland Jubilee Singers.

After Paul Exkano left in 1952 to return to the ministry, the Alabama Blind Boys reached their performing peak with a series of classic recordings for Speciality, joined for a while by Rev Percell Perkins from the Mississippi Blind Boys. While they never quite matched their Mississippi counterparts, neither artistically nor in terms of popular acclaim, they were nevertheless a major force among the hard gospel quartets largely due to the savagely commanding voice of Clarence Fountain ... a screamer of epic proportions. After a spell with Savoy Records in the sixties, the Original Blind Boys of Alabama gradually lost their hard edge, eventually reduced to singing dispirited versions of songs like *Danny Boy*. Humiliation and indignity were regular burdens heaped on the back of gospel groups, never sadder than when self-inflicted. They reformed though in the 80s, initially to tour with the musical *Gospel At Colonus*, restoring the group to form and finally bringing a new respect and material rewards commensurate with their artistry. In 1995, they released a fine album recorded at the House of Blues in Los Angeles and a whole new lease of life currently beckons for Clarence Fountain and the guys from Talladega.

During the 1940s and 1950s there were far more exceptional quartets than a book like this can possibly do justice to. Rev Sam McCrary led the great Fairfield Four out of Nashville during those two decades, but he was also their front man (boy) in their original 1921 line-up at the age of seven and occupied the same position in the re-activated group until his death in 1987, when his duties as pastor of St Mark's Baptist Church in Nashville allowed. The Fairfields have today followed the Alabama Blind Boys out onto the world concert circuit and are finally seeing pay-days that approximate to justice. The Jubalaires took gospel quartet into the rock 'n' roll era, appearing in several Elvis Presley films and with people like Ry Cooder. The Chosen Gospel Singers were a fine, emotional quartet with Lou Rawls and Joe Hinton in their early line-up, eventually changing their name to the Gospel Keynotes in the mid-1960s when they began featuring the stratospheric voice of the young Paul Beasley. The Pilgrim Travelers were possibly the first gospel quartet to be heavily promoted and they earned huge sums for Specialty Records from 1948 onwards. Like the famous Soul Stirrers (see Chapter 5) they hailed from Texas and copied many of their stylings, but they had the powerful voices of Kylo Turner and Jess Whittaker, and the management skills of the great J. W. Alexander to carry them through. From Richmond in Virginia came the Harmonizing Four with their polar opposite to the star falsettos of other groups - the incredible bass voice of Jimmy Jones. And so many others - the Paramount Singers, the Selah Singers, the Flying Clouds of Detroit, the Swanee Quintet, the Highway QC's, the Pilgrim Jubilees, the Bells of Joy ....

The era of male group dominance of gospel began to be challenged towards the end of the 1940s with the emergence of their female counterparts, usually singing three-part harmony arrangements. By the middle of the 1950s, the male quartets were in rapid decline and only a tiny handful survived on into the 1960s with anything like the success of their hey-day.

From out of the heart of the deep South came the Angelic Gospel Singers - Margaret Allison, Lucille Shird, Josephine McDowell and Ella Mae Norris. Their downhome versions of the old hymns and gospel tunes, loosely sung to piano and sometimes organ accompaniment, turned them into one of Gotham Records' hottest properties in the early 1950s. Some of the earliest records were as joint ventures with the Dixie Hummingbirds and they formed a popular double bill for many years with songs like *Standing Out On The Highway* and *Jesus Will Answer Prayer*.

In the North at about the same time, the ill-fated Davis Sisters were beginning to rise to prominence. An initial line-up had Ruth Davis, her sisters Audrey, Thelma and Alfreda, Imogene Greene and Curtis Dublin on piano. Imogene Green, a childhood friend of James Cleveland, stayed for only a few years, later replaced by Jackie Verdell, a contemporary of Aretha Franklin. At the height of their fame the Davis Sisters rivalled the Ward Singers and were one of the young Jessy Dixon's great idols,

"I remember when the Davis Sisters sang - there were five ladies and one man at the piano - but they sounded like a choir. They didn't have to hover round the microphone, they stood way back and directed their voices to it. That was some of the best singing that the world has ever known."

Photo: Terry Cryer.

Clara Ward and the Ward Singers at the
100 Club in London, 1959.

Their seemingly limitless vocal power might have put them at the very top but they were continuously dogged by tragedy - no less than four of the group's singers met with untimely deaths. One Davis Sister was burned to death in a horrific accident but the story of Ruth 'Baby Sis' Davis, is perhaps the saddest of all. In her prime she thundered forth with consummate ease, her lustrous contralto as hard as nails, but she was dragged down physically by diabetes and by the kidney and liver disease that finally killed her in 1970, a veritable shadow of her former self.

At the National Baptist Convention in 1943, Mother Gertrude Ward of Philadelphia introduced her 14-year old daughter Clara, and caused a sensation that carried through two decades. The fabulous Ward Singers were far and away the most successful female group of gospel's golden age, tearing up churches by the hundred with an intoxicating repertoire of old Watts' hymns matched with the pick of the new Dorsey and Brewster songs.

Clara Ward was the star of the group and star is definitely the right word. Acutely aware of her ability to shout an audience by moaning a hymn like *The Day is Past and Gone* or *Amazing Grace*, she became ever more flamboyant in both dress and manner until it all became an elaborate spectacle. People went wild for it and turned the Wards into a travelling phenomenon.

> *"They were like the Supremes," smiled Jessy Dixon. "They wore fabulous gowns and they travelled in this long limousine with a trailer on the back that carried their costumes. They would go to different churches on Sunday mornings and sing just one song and then announce that they would be back that evening. At night you wouldn't be able to get near the place because all the people would have telephoned around to say that the Ward Singers were in town - it was like an underground movement."*

At their peak during the 1950s they were the ultimate female gospel stylists, blessed with a vocal chorus that for eleven years included the illustrious voice of Marion Williams. The Clara Ward spectacle and charisma drew the crowds, but it was Marion who increasingly took over the job of delivering the goods. It's her voice on the Ward Singers' million-selling hits - *Surely God Is Able* and *Packin' Up* - soaring up from growling blues to a staggeringly high soprano. Clara could still slay them with the odd hymn or two and her fame was so great that she was still able to beat Mahalia Jackson into second place in the polls, but Marion's was the voice that dominated the group now.

It is the fate of almost every gospel singer - Mahalia Jackson apart - to be largely unrecognised by the world except for what they gave to popular music by proxy. So Rev Claude Jeter is re-invented as Al Green and Clara Ward is continuously disinterred by Aretha Franklin. Marion Williams, one of the last great contralto voices from gospel's golden age, was recast in mutant form by Little Richard (and the Isley Brothers) who parodied her trademark whoops and hollers and who in turn passed them, burlesque fashion, to The Beatles.

Her life's work was infinitely more significant. Born in 1927 to poor Miami parents active in local gospel choirs, she learned to sing as a child in her neighbourhood Church of God. Following her father's early death, she was sent out to work at nine years old - menial and service jobs to support her family. Her reputation meanwhile as a gifted church singer, grew beyond her native Florida and her break came when, at the age of twenty, she was recruited by Clara Ward. As the nascent star of the Famous Ward Singers, Marion Williams

Photo: Val Wilmer.

Marion Williams autographs Black Nativity albums
at Dobell's Jazz Record Shop in London, 1969.

eventually came to overshadow the imperious Clara and, by 1958, was sufficiently disenchanted by Clara's artistic and financial exploitation to lead a walk-out of group members. "*It's a sit-down strike*" declared Clara, her own glory days effectively over, soon to decamp for Las Vegas and ignominy.

During her eleven years with the Ward Singers, Marion Williams came to rival Mahalia Jackson herself around America's gospel circuit and enjoyed million-selling hits, among them W. H. Brewster's classic hymn *Surely God Is Able*. She was poised for greater recognition and achieved it with her new group The Stars of Faith and the phenomenal success of the stage musical in which they starred with Alex Bradford. Langston Hughes' *Black Nativity* was the first gospel musical and an unlikely Broadway hit. In 1962 the show transferred to London and Marion Williams continued to entrance critics and public alike.

Black Nativity, and Marion's interpretation of songs like *A Pity and a Shame* and *When Was Jesus Born,* exposed her to the new audience for jazz and blues, who became adoring converts to her flawless, southern contralto, if not to her faith. When she began a solo recording career in 1965, she attracted sidemen as diverse as Milt Jackson and Keith Jarrett and was in constant demand on the American college circuit. Awards and acclaim followed, but commercial success always eluded her and her later years were divided between occasional concerts and the Holiness Church in Boston, where she became pastor, commuting 400 miles from her Philadelphia home.

Such rewards and enticements as were on offer to Marion during her life usually came with unacceptable secular strings attached. More than a decade ago she was offered $100,000 to desert gospel for rhythm and blues. It met with an entirely typical response (and a fitting epitaph): "*I told 'em the church is in my system. I'll live and die a gospel singer.*" And so she did - at home in Philadelphia in July 1994.

Towards the end of the 1950s, when the Ward Singers were the undisputed queens of gospel, Clara pushed the group to undignified extremes, decking them out in bizarre wigs and showy outfits, milking her massive reputation for all it was worth. "*There were occasions,*" remembers Madeleine Bell, "*when people turned up to see the Clara Ward Singers and Clara wouldn't even be there. It got so that she had three or four different groups and they were all called the Ward Singers. If you were an agent you had to specify you wanted Clara and the Ward Singers or you didn't get her. I remember she was a very small woman, Clara Ward. She was thin but she was not thick!*"

In 1958, the main group including Marion Williams finally made their move and quit to become the Stars of Faith. Clara, scarcely daunted, quickly regrouped and went all the way into show business. In 1961 she scandalised the churches by signing a 40-week contract with a Las Vegas nightclub to do mock gospel routines for a fee of $200,000. They re-signed her for another 40 weeks and then another until she was finally as tragic as Las Vegas itself. She died on 16th January 1973, when she was still only 48 - a bizarre self-parody at the end, but a great gospel adventuress in her time. "*I watched her carry gospel into many, many places where it hadn't been before and where it hasn't been since ...,*" said her old friend James Cleveland, adding "*Giants fall and little chips grow. Many young persons who were inspired by her as I was, will pick up and carry on like Clara would have wanted them to.*"

If the Wards' mantle of female supergroup was passed to any of the little chips in gospel it must be considered to have passed to the legendary Caravans. Though other fine groups followed more directly in Clara's footsteps - Chicago's great Barrett Sisters or the Imperial Gospel Singers from Philadelphia's Christian Hope Baptist Church for instance - few female gospel acts had that same star quality written all over them the way the Caravans had.

Organised originally in 1952 as the backing chorus for Robert Anderson (striking out on his own after leaving the Roberta Martin Singers), their early recordings for States Records focussed on the powerful lead voice of Albertina Walker on traditional songs like *What A Friend We Have In Jesus* and *Blessed Assurance*. When the famed contralto, Bessie Griffin, moved up from her native New Orleans to join the Caravans in Chicago, Albertina stepped aside to let Bessie lead on most songs, including *Since I Met Jesus* and *Ain't That Good News*. Putting Bessie out front was Albertina's tactical ploy to gain national attention but it didn't work out and Bessie moved on to continue seeking the recognition she deserved but never did receive.

As Bessie Griffin moved out, the young James Cleveland, rising composer and arranger for Roberta Martin's *Studio of Music*, moved in. The new Cleveland arrangements were distinctly hot and classy, propelling the Caravans into the avant garde of gospel and attracting a rush of phenomenal young singers - Cassietta George joined in 1955, followed by Dorothy Norwood, Inez Andrews and Imogene Greene from the Davis Sisters. The surfeit of vocal talent made for a volatile group existence and the Caravans were always an explosive unit. When properly motivated, they sparked one another into compelling antiphony but personal and money problems forever intruded. The great voices came and went.

Albertina was always there, leading the way, and the hugely popular Inez Andrews - a statuesque Alabaman with the most uniquely melodic shriek in the whole of gospel - stayed for about five years. Madeleine Bell was with the Alex Bradford Singers at that time and has vivid memories of Inez:

> "We did a couple of programmes with the Caravans and I remember her singing lead - she had an amazing voice. She was about six feet tall, very thin and I can picture her standing on stage at the Apollo Theatre leaning on the Hammond organ - she was eight and a half months pregnant - singing Oh Mary Don't You Weep, and I cried. I could not believe this woman."

With evangelical dynamite added to the Caravans in the shape of the diminutive Shirley Caesar, the group was unbeatable on the road. Shirley had the task of opening the show and roused the audience to fever pitch, hurling graphic sermonettes at them like an old time preacher. By the time Inez and Albertina came to the front of the stage, the house was already in uproar. Not surprisingly, Shirley wasn't content to be the little warm-up girl for long and when Inez left in 1961, she seized her promotion and effectively took the Caravans through their peak years with her big crowd pleasers - *Comfort Me, Hallelujah, It's Done, Running For Jesus*, and *Sweeping Through The City*.

Not even the Caravans could hold Shirley for long though and after she left in 1967 to concentrate on evangelism, Albertina found herself deserted by all the rest a few months later. She pulled in new members but the magic was gone and she eventually resigned herself to the solo role that her proteges had all chosen. As a skillful organiser she threw herself into Chicago politics, working with Rev Jesse Jackson and organising the Operation PUSH People's Choir. For a time she restricted her appearances to special occasions, like the Caravans' Twentieth Anniversary Celebrations, when she was honoured by no less than eighteen singers who had all, at some time, been privileged to serve in the group she'd struggled so long to hold together. For once it seems there's a happier ending and Albertina Walker, the woman who launched more gospel careers out of one group than anyone else, is now at last finding her own mass audience and ironically rivalling Shirley Caesar for the title 'Queen of Gospel'.

Numerically, the male quartets always dominated the golden age but there were many female groups travelling the same hard road. All through the years when Albertina Walker's flock ruled the roost and back further through the heyday of the Ward Singers, Dorothy Love Coates and the Original Gospel Harmonettes were perhaps the main female challenge to their twin supremacy.

Dorothy is fiercely uncompromising and with good reason. She was a lone female voice in the Alabama heartland of male quartet and married twice directly into it - first, briefly, to Willie Love of the Fairfield Four, then much later to Carl Coates of the Sensational Nightingales. The Original Gospel Harmonettes were Birmingham's great female counterpart to the stentorian excellence of its finest sons, but Dorothy was always way ahead of them. While they harmonised with precision and restraint she declaimed with extreme urgency, pushing herself physically to the limit.

She spent two long periods as leader of the Gospel Harmonettes, taking a three-year break in 1959. The rigours of the gospel life, the punishment she imposed on herself through performance and the miseries inflicted by southern racism were constantly attacking her spirit. She never let any of it beat her. When the Civil Rights movement swept the South, she threw herself into the local campaigns of Martin Luther King, marched the streets of Birmingham and sang at fund-raising benefits. When she returned to gospel with a reorganised Harmonettes, her abrasive spirit was more than re-charged and she captured a mass audience with defiant lyrics of faith and struggle:

> *Old Satan is busy stirring up wrath, gathering stones to block my path.*
> *Enemies inflicting all the hurt they can, throwing their rocks and hiding their hands.*
> *If you dig one ditch you better dig two; the trap you set just might be for you.*
> *He put it in my heart, you can't change me, my soul's on fire, and the world can't harm me.*

Hers was never the sweetest voice in gospel but she spoke a greater truth than most. Where others were as docile off stage as they were frenetic on, Dorothy lived out her righteousness to the full, commanding a special kind of respect from her audiences. Without any of the Wards' clowning or costumes or hairdos, she rivalled their popularity by becoming a trusted spokeswoman and a heartfelt performer. There is a specific injustice in the comparative obscurity of Dorothy Love Coates and the Gospel Harmonettes.

With any number of small aggregations blanketing the country throughout the 1940s and 1950s, it might seem that there was little room for solo gospel singers but they had their niches too. Mahalia Jackson of course ploughed her own furrow with spectacular success, but singers like Madame Edna Gallman Cooke found a big southern audience with her country sermonettes on Nashboro Records, Bessie Griffin might have been the greatest of all but she was cheated every step of the way, Brother Joe May had a huge following for his rocking gospel blues, the Reverend Cleophus Robinson packed them into his Greater

Photos:
Viv Broughton/Ray Funk.

Top, Dorothy Love and Carl Coates, 1995. Below, The Gospel Harmonettes (Dorothy standing at rear) and The Sensational Nightingales (Julius Cheeks, front right, Carl Coates, rear left).

Bethlehem Baptist Church in St Louis through the 50s and 60s and sold prodigiously for Peacock, Mother Mattie Moss Clark's albums for Savoy achieved gold status but she's been wilfully neglected by historians; Professor Charles Taylor, Reverend Robert Ballinger, Delois Barret-Campbell - all built their followings.

Inevitably, they tended to be somewhat eccentric, even by gospel's broad standards - iron willed characters who were too brash, too stubborn or too unique for subordination into someone else's group. Sister Rosetta Tharpe, preceding even Mahalia Jackson, was forever her own woman and her music defied all of gospel's categorisation. Essentially a Holiness singer, she nevertheless exuded jollity rather than passion and her rollicking guitar-based gospel is quite unmistakable "Rosetta was a great inspiration to me," Inez Andrews recalled. "She used to tease me all the time and say, "Come on Inez, you can do it!" I couldn't see no woman picking no guitar like she did, but she did it, and with a lot of grace and dignity."

She was born Rosetta Nubin in Cotton Plant, Arkansas and debuted as 'Little Sister' with her mother Katie Bell up in Chicago at the age of six, singing I Looked Down The Line And I Wondered to an audience of a thousand. The song turned up on her first Decca recordings in 1938 and she was instantly the brightest new star in gospel.

Moving to New York, her jazz affinities and stylings attracted sinners as much as saints and she took a plum job with the Cab Calloway Orchestra where her rousing, foot-stomping spirituals found an unlikely home. Didn't It Rain, Up Above My Head I Hear Music In The Air and Strange Things Are Happening Every Day have become jazz classics every bit as much as gospel gems and she somehow managed to keep a foot firmly in each camp for much of her long career. Listening to her now, it's easy to see why the jazz fraternity were happy to take a little religion with her music but quite how she got away with recording I Want A Tall Skinny Papa, rip up the clubs all week and still face a church crowd on Sunday remains a mystery.

By the time gospel's golden age was beginning to roll, Rosetta had temporarily given up the double life and was back with the church exclusively. Teaming up with Marie Knight, a young singer from Oakwood Avenue Baptist Church in Newark, Sister Rosetta Tharpe became one of the great attractions on the gospel circuit, drawing huge crowds - 17,000 to a song-fest in Ponce de Leon Park in Atlanta, 27,000 to Griffith Stadium, Washington DC in 1950 and capacity audiences elsewhere in every State. When she married in 1951, the open-air gospel wedding attracted a phenomenal 25,000 paying guests!

She could do no wrong, or so she thought, but uproar followed a blues recording she did with Marie and the two split up - Marie for a chance at pop success which failed badly, consigning her finally to a job as a Brooklyn telephone operator; Rosetta to face the wrath of churches who had forgiven past indiscretions but were more resolute now. She suffered badly this time, the more so because in her heart she was still solidly with gospel. It got so she had no option but to move into Mahalia's orbit - playing the international concert circuit to mainly white audiences, who came for the music but not the message.

Up to her death in 1973, Sister Rosetta came to personify gospel to the rest of the world almost as much as Mahalia Jackson did, but she was never typical of the gospel mainstream. Like another guitar evangelist, Elder Utah Smith (famous for his amazing I Got Two Wings), Rosetta created a hybrid music, a fusion of swing jazz and jumping spirituals. There has certainly never been anyone quite like her, before or since.

Sister Rosetta Tharpe, guitarist, singer and performer extraordinary;
Inset: poster for one of her many Apollo shows in New York.

Gospel's always been full of people who didn't quite fit the mould. Bessemer in Alabama for instance, was renowned for its sensational quartets and any local guy with half a voice would fight tooth and nail for a place in the Kings of Harmony or the Blue Jays or the Swan Silvertones or any of a score of others. Yet in that steel town there was still Prophet Jones, bedecked in gorgeous robes, playing piano with his feet, who in turn inspired the young Alex Bradford to become everyone's favourite gospel showman through the 1950s and 1960s.

Immediately post-war, Bradford (as he became known to all and sundry) shipped himself out of Alabama and into Chicago, where Mahalia and Roberta Martin reigned supreme. Roberta, regally introduced him at a programme. "So I got up, and they'd never heard a man make all those high soprano notes before. Baby, they were carrying folks out bodily." In the mid-1950s he formed the very first all-male gospel group (as opposed to quartet) - the Bradford Specials - stunning the gospel circuit with falsetto approximations of the Wards' material and a jaw-dropping line in choreography. Signed by Speciality in a rash moment, they suddenly hit with Bradford's own song and subsequent gospel classic *Too Close To Heaven*. It sold well over a million copies and Bradford camped it up all over as the 'singing rage of the gospel age'.

By the end of the 1950s he was using the occasional female voice in his group and Madeleine Bell joined him out of the Glovertones in 1960, touring Europe with him in *Black Nativity*. His oblique training techniques and prodigious musical knowledge had earned him the title of 'Professor' Bradford:

> *"He taught me just about everything I know as far as singing goes. One time we travelled 2,000 miles by bus from New York to New Orleans for a programme and when I got there I lost my voice - couldn't speak a word, but he taught me how you can sing right over that even though you still can't speak. And the volume I got from him. I'd sing as loud as I could but he'd come up behind me at rehearsals and punch me hard in the back - I trebled my volume and he said, 'sing like that all the time - just think I'm going to come up behind you and punch you in the back if you don't'. And I still think of that now."*

On the road, the hardest thing for artists was getting money out of promoters - no less for gospel singers than any other. Bradford's temper was legendary and he had his own way of dealing with those who crossed him. Madeleine Bell again:

> *"One time we were on stage and Bradford suddenly couldn't see the promoter. He was off after him in a flash, leaving us still singing. Caught the man red-handed, climbing out the window with the money-bag in his hand. When he died, my mother tried to go to the funeral in New York but she couldn't even get into the block. So many people turned out, the whole block round the church was roped off."*

There's precious little room now in gospel for eccentric genius in the Bradford mould. As the electric age came down over the music like an avenging angel, singers and choirs, songwriters and publishers, quartets and gospel groups all adapted to its conforming influence or died resisting it. Mostly they died. A religious folk-art founded entirely on the human voice and acoustic music, doesn't sit gracefully alongside an amplified back-beat and a show-time band. Rhythm and blues may have been great dance music but it proved for a long time to be a lousy bedfellow of gospel, inflicting many of its lesser talents on the hapless groups under record company pressure to modernise. Don Robey at Peacock, with a

Dorothy Norwood, graduate of The Caravans.

heavy **R&B** rosta as well as the cream of gospel quartets, began to insist that all gospel recordings included at least a drummer and preferably a full band. Other companies - Vee Jay for instance - even over-dubbed drums and bass onto gospel tracks after they had been recorded.

Under the onslaught of cheap, badly recorded rhythm sections it seems that solo voices survived easier than groups and women fared better than men - perhaps because the female voice was more naturally able to ring out over the noise. So the Caravans (and their graduates like Shirley Caesar) and the Loving Sisters, added an **R&B** backing to gospel successfully while the Swanee Quintet drowned in the attempt.

The male groups who did survive were the young bloods coming in at the end of the long quartet tradition. Sharp dressers and hard screamers, they met **R&B** head on and matched it for tearing excitement - exceeded it even. Sometimes they also produced music as compelling as any in gospel's golden age. The Gospelaires of Dayton, Ohio were one of the most exciting of the young male groups with a harmonic range and vocal intensity that is almost inconceivable today. Founded by Melvyn Pullen, Clarence Kendricks and the ecstatic Paul Arnold in 1954, they were virtually unbeatable in the late 1950s and early 1960s with a front rank that included Arnold, ultra-high tenor Charles McLean and the almost gutteral ragings of Robert Washington. Recording exclusively for Peacock Records with brilliant guitarist Robert Lattimore, they contributed a series of definitive hard gospel performances, including the magnum opus - *Remember Me Jesus*. If I were forced to pick just two records out of the whole of gospel music this would be one of them, for it captures the passion and vocal perfections of gospel most completely. Only once did I see them in person and then without Robert Washington, but they almost laid me out for a week.

"The Mighty Clouds of Joy have been together for about twenty-five years and we're totally dedicated to it. We've had so many offers to go commercial you know ... if we'd have gone into singing rock and roll, we'd be millionaires several times over, but gospel's in my blood and we'll keep on until they listen." Willie Joe Ligon sat in a West London hotel room and reflected on more than thirty years at the helm of one of the few hard gospel quartets to survive successfully into the present day. *"I started this group when I was fourteen years old and my big inspiration was Rev Julius Cheecks of the Sensational Nightingales. I went to a concert they did in Los Angeles and he became a kind of father figure."*

Young Joe Ligon had moved to LA from Troy in Alabama where he was born, bringing with him the urgency of southern church singing and pitching it against the more sophisticated city voice of California-born Johnny Martin. The two lead voices then added bassman Richard Wallace from rural Georgia and baritone Elmo Franklin from Florida, and began to sing at small church events around the poorer parts of booming Los Angeles. Soon after, Elmo's brother Ermant joined them and also became their first manager, together with two new members - Leon Polk and David Walker. A single radio programme, broadcast over a local Watts radio station in 1959 was their debut proper, recorded but not issued until nine years later when Hob Records in their wisdom chose to dub in organ, piano and drums to songs like *Amazing Grace* and *Take Me To The Water*.

Within a few months, they got their own recording break and the original seven members of the Mighty Clouds travelled down to the Goldstar Studios in Houston, Texas. Word of their great vocal prowess had reached the ears of Don Robey, who was looking to beef up his ailing catalogue of older quartets. He'd

Photos: Viv Broughton/Author's collection.

Joe Ligon and (inset) the Mighty Clouds of Joy.

already made a killing out of the Five Blind Boys, the Nightingales and the Dixie Hummingbirds, but those days were nearly over and only the Gospelaires showed any chance of repeating that kind of success and, as he once joked, the Clouds were going to be his 'silver lining'. The day was 28th September 1960 and the two songs they recorded that day for their very first single were *Jesus Lead Us Safely* and *Ain't Got Long Here*. Both songs appeared subsequently on the debut album *Family Circle* a couple of years later.

For ten years they painstakingly built their reputation as the hardest male gospel group on the road, employing all the vocal weapons in the quartet armoury and dressing them up in a devastating show of youthful charisma. Sporting exaggerated pompadour hairstyles and slick mohair suits they descended on one town after another and left audiences reeling from their wildly emotional performances of songs and sermonettes.

A Bright Side is their archetypal sermonette - a hair-raising tale of mother/son tragedy in the classic shouting preacher style, that has all the Clouds stretched to their limit, over hovering organ and guitar chords. With Joe Ligon roaring and screaming, forcing the group up higher and higher, it scales a peak of intensity that is almost frightening. *"When we recorded that in 1964,"* Joe remembered, *"We put out a call over the radio station and got people to come on down to the studio so we could do it live and get some church going. Just one take we did it in."*

The Clouds have been virtually full-time on the road since then, rarely doing less than 200 shows a year, sharing stages and touring the world with everyone from Andrae Crouch to the Rolling Stones and Earth, Wind and Fire. In the mid-1970s, the Clouds were on the verge of following the Staple Singers into the gentler pastures of 'inspirational music' - soul with a minimum of stirring. Johnny Martin was pumping it up in the wake of a bitter split with Don Robey's Peacock Records and a prestigious new deal with ABC:

> *"We intend to go right to the top as an R & B group,"* he told one writer. *"See, we've all been around a long time, and we've done our fair share of dues-paying on the gospel circuit. It wasn't until 1963 that we could even afford to stay in hotels. When we were on the road, we just had to sleep in our van. People just seem to play gospel music cheap. The thing we recently found ourselves in with Peacock was a living example of the Lord moving in mysterious ways. Ever since we signed with that company, we had been doing most of our own writing, producing and arranging, but it wasn't until about three years ago we discovered how much they'd been ripping us off for. You see, although we've all been around for a long time, we were pretty naive when it came to being hip to publishing rights and that type of stuff. So we took our contracts to a lawyer for his advice, and he nearly flipped. He described the terms as "slavery". He was right too, because all that time we had been getting just one-eighth of a penny on what we had written, and we'd been steady selling albums for fifteen years! So we took out a lawsuit against the company, and it was around that time that ABC took over. We figured we were finished then because we had gotten pretty cold, no new releases for three years. But the vice-president, Otis Smith, was hip enough to realise that even without new stuff on the market, we were still selling more than some of their established artists. He introduced us to Dave Crawford, who just gathered together a pile of our old albums and disappeared. When we next saw him, he'd written a whole set of new material for us. They didn't need to talk us into recording more commercial sounding stuff, we were all for the idea, because we saw it as a way of getting our message which was, is, and always will be, the word of God, to a far wider audience. The younger generation for example, a lot of the kids in our black ghettoes are in pretty bad shape with*

the drugs thing and crime. Those are the people who need some kind of spiritual guidance and we weren't really reaching them before. To get to them you have to wrap your message in an R&B sound."

But Alex Bradford, for one, was distinctly less enthusiastic about the new ways of selling the music:

"You know those little men that sit up in their ivory towers and decide what is going to be a hit next month. They have raped gospel for 25 years trying to kill it. Now ABC is going for it, but they want to prostitute it still. They don't want you to say anything about Jesus or God. They want you to be negative, but if you take the feeling away from it, you got nothing but a plastic kind of thing."

For a while there in the mid-1970s it looked like Bradford's prediction was going to be the Clouds' reality. They hovered right on the brink of commercial success in the big league and appeared to capitulate to the claims it made on them. The now-familiar ambiguity over lyrics crept in, so that any one track could be taken either as a romantic love song or as a song of divine adoration. Now, someone like Al Green could get away with this because he was clearly perceived as travelling from pop deeper into religion, but if the movement appears to be in the opposite direction - away from gospel and closer to pop - then the motives of the artist are liable to be called into question. The Mighty Clouds began to look, then, as if they were carefully hedging their bets, preparing to drop gospel altogether and go for gold.

No doubt they could have done it too, but something drew them back into gospel proper. Despite R&B hits like *Time* and *Ride The Mighty High* and the prospect of a phenomenal secular career ahead of them, they chose to get back off the fence on the less profitable side. Even so they were doing pretty well. Their recording of *Live And Direct* earned them a gold album and they won Grammy Awards in 1978 and 1980, with plaudits coming thick and fast - *'no singing group on the face of the earth produces a more joyful sound.'*

These days, Joe Ligon doesn't strain his vocal chords in quite the way he used to, preferring to share the lead duties with new members - for a while it was Paul Beasley, the amazingly high-voiced singer from the Gospel Keynotes. Nevertheless, he's still regarded as one of the greatest male singers to have survived into the present day. At the 1995 Gospel Music Workshop of America *Quartet Night* in Los Angeles, Joe as elder statesman took his place on stage alongside five southern sons, The Christianaires, who are successfully re-inventing the genre, tearing up the room in the style of the original Clouds of Joy. A few years back, I watched the Mighty Clouds in front of European audiences during a tour that included a capacity crowd of 30,000 at the Greenbelt Festival. It was quite something to stand among that vast throng of youthful Christians and feel them respond, first in awe and disbelief, then in roaring, shouting support with the whole crowd jumping several feet into the air.

I realised then, looking out over the thousands of bobbing heads in the cold night air, that there were probably no more than a handful of people out of that entire audience with the merest inkling of gospel's long hard journey. Even among the new generation of gospel fans, following John P. Kee or Anointed or BeBe and CeCe Winans, there is little recognition that the Mighty Clouds of Joy - and other current stars like Shirley Caesar - are the last surviving links in a chain stretching right back through Gospel's Golden Age.

It's a whole new programme now. ❖

Brother Joe May, the Thunderbolt of the Mid West, with his children.

Photo: Specialty Records.

YOU'D BETTER RUN ON

The Original Soul Music of America

"We have a lot of rock-and-roll singers out in the audience," the gospel singer Inez Andrews said over the telephone from New Orleans last Sunday. *"They come purposely to see what they can learn - or what they can steal. They'll come backstage and say, 'Hey, girl, I've got to know what you did on those last eight bars.' Rock-and-Roll singers steal even worse than the gospel singers. Because we had something to steal from the very beginning, while they had nothing."*
New York Times - Friday, 9th March 1979

One Sunday in Gary, Indiana a few years later, Stevie Wonder turned up unannounced with Deniece Williams at her local church. Sitting down at the piano he began to sing *Have a Talk With God* to the congregation but, finding the piano badly out of tune, switched over to the church organ.

"He was jamming on that organ too, man. He made it sound like a synthesiser and stuff. He can't even see and he made it sound like a synthesiser. And he swayed back and forth like this here. Then the choir - there were three choirs and they turned it into a mass choir - sang Oh Happy Day and he was leading the

solo. And my cousin was playing organ and another dude was playing drums, and after church they were trying to get that contract!" Stevie later gave them a new piano.

The familiar route from gospel obscurity to secular acclaim is not quite as well-worn as legend would like to have it. Even at the peak of the soul music boom in the 1960s, when record company men looked on the African-American churches the way oil men looked on the North Sea, there were always twenty exquisite voices who stayed behind for every one that left. This book is mostly by way of tribute to those who stayed, but it would be a perverse history that ignored the impact of gospel music on popular culture. Besides, the biblical injunction about the minority who stray is appropriate here. Faith is sustained by the many who keep it, but it's also given urgency by those who don't.

Most people approach the gospel/soul nexus as complete outsiders - familiar with the resolutely public face of soul music, curious perhaps about the church confines from whence it came. More than thirty years ago, when Sam Cooke was enjoying the first flush of commercial success, I chanced on the first recordings in church of the fourteen-year-old and, at that stage, completely unknown Aretha Franklin. The fervent outpourings of such a young girl as she extemporised on the old Watts and Dorsey hymns, was a stunning revelation and sparked a journey of exploration into the roots of soul. It didn't take long to discover that the view is very different for those on the inside looking out.

The gospel church is a church that defends its children like a lioness. The fellowships of young people are clutched tight to the bosom of Abraham, schooled in Baptist or Pentecostal mystique, subject to strict codes of discipline over dress and behaviour. It's rarely brutal or unlovely though and most who grew up under its brooding tutelage turn wistful at memories of getting dressed up in 'Sunday going-to-meeting clothes' for church outings and family occasions.

"I can remember those church picnics like it was yesterday," says one ex-gospel singer, *"They were such real happy times for us kids and though we used to kick against the rules, I can see now that it was the church that kept us out of trouble. If we hadn't been in the church we'd have been just hanging around the streets, getting picked up by the police. The church had us so busy with the Lord's work, there wasn't no time left to get into trouble."*

Music holds a peculiar fascination for young people in the church, not least because it flirts with secular temptation. Ever since Thomas Dorsey married off blues and spirituals to create gospel, the sights and sounds of African-American church music have influenced those of secular music, and vice versa. The sense of danger generated thereby, is one of the great attractions of gospel music for teenagers. Despite the familiar claim that 'when you join the gospel Church, you don't stop dancing, you just change partners', it remains an area of considerable tension. Just where devotive worship leaves off and sensual pleasure begins is anyone's guess, but the elders and the pastors will draw arbitrary lines and stick to them. Music that entices pubescent youth is subject to the same kind of church law enforcement as the other pleasures of the flesh - permissable only if divinely inspired and in their rightful Christian context. Musical virtue is as fiercely protected as any other virtue in the gospel churches.

For many though, it is this very inclusion of temporal pleasures into the religious sphere that makes the

African-American church so down to earth and full of humanity. There's no false asceticism and worship is an exuberant collective experience that extends over long periods. It's a form of therapy for the soul, healing the wounds inflicted on it by the heartlessness of the world. James Baldwin's oft quoted description of a store front service, captures it: '... we *all became equal, wringing wet, singing and dancing, in anguish and rejoicing, at the foot of the altar.*' Strength regained didn't always become power realised, but the resurgent qualities of gospel music sustained the saints through two centuries of bondage and oppression. From this perspective it may now seem that out of such strength cometh forth ... well, weakness would perhaps be too extreme, but a diminution certainly. The forms of gospel - the chord changes, the call-and-response, the melismatic styles - are evident in soul music, but the incredible passion and power is watered down to facilitate the cross-over.

Sam Cooke is the classic case. Along with Dinah Washington (who began her singing career as Ruth Jones in the 1940s with Sallie Martin), Sam Cooke was one of the most important figures in the transition from gospel to soul. He was born in Clarksdale, Mississippi but the family of eight joined the great migration up to Chicago in the early 1930s, just like Dorsey and Sallie Martin and Mahalia Jackson and all the other gospel pioneers. Father Charles became a Baptist minister and by 1940, Sam had his first taste of gospel with the Singing Children - a family group that appropriately enough included his two sisters and a brother. When Rev C. S. Cook (Sam added the 'e' to his last name later) moved to the pastorate of Chicago's Highway Baptist Church, the teenagers organised themselves as the Highway QCs under the guidance of R. B. Robinson, who was at that stage baritone singer with one of the most famous gospel quartets of all time - the Soul Stirrers.

The history of the Soul Stirrers is a book in itself. They were formed in Texas around 1934 and were already breaking out of the straitjacket of traditional jubilee quartet. Even back in 1936 when they were still working as farm hands, the veteran folklorist Alan Lomax was recording them for the Library of Congress and remembered being overwhelmed by "*the most incredible polyrhythmic stuff you've ever heard.*" The last surviving member of that original group was Jesse Farley who recalled: "*Back then, we took things as they came. I can remember one time in 1936, the Soul Stirrers held a revival in this all-coloured town, Boley, Oklahoma. Do you know, the whole group made two dollars sixty five for the entire week? But nobody was married, everybody was young, the fellows wanted to travel.*"

Their first time into Chicago created a huge stir in gospel circles. Not only were they applying the Southern quartet style to the Thomas Dorsey songs (*Precious Lord* was early in their programme) but they had also introduced the most revolutionary development in harmony group history - the use of a second lead voice, allowing the first to stand prominent and be a focal point. The innovation may not seem so extraordinary now, but it opened up the way for all the great lead voices of quartet to come through. Julius Cheeks, Ira Tucker, Claude Jeter, Archie Brownlee et al, were each allowed to break through into the creative space invented by the Stirrers.

Within the Stirrers themselves, the man who made the greatest use of that space was Rebert H. Harris. His contribution to gospel quartet is quite phenomenal. Almost all the trademarks of the modern quartet style are traceable to Harris - the lyrical ad libs, the delayed time signatures, the antiphony and especially falsetto leads. "*Even women didn't sing falsetto in church back then,*" he often declares.

Photos: Ray Funk.

The legendary Soul Stirrers. Main picture: In performance, with Sam Cooke. Inset: The Highway QCs with Sam Cooke.
Top right: The Soul Stirrers, pre Sam Cooke, in the early 1940s. Below right: Rebert H. Harris.

Harris epitomised the new wave of quartet lead and his work with the Soul Stirrers was widely imitated. Sam Cooke was heavily under the Harris spell himself, appearing with the Highway QCs on the same bill as the Stirrers and other quartets like the Blind Boys of Mississippi and the Pilgrim Travellers. During the late 1940s, quartet had become exceptionally popular and a moral laxity had subsequently infected the circuit - even to the extent of female groupies following the male groups around for casual affairs. R. H. Harris was raised to carry himself with integrity and this new thing wasn't his style at all. *"I believe there's this virtue that goes along with gospel. There's more to it than good singing. It's a beaconing thing that other folk can see without you talking it."* In 1950 Harris quit the Soul Stirrers *"because the moral aspects of the thing just fell out into the water. The singers didn't care anything about it. They felt they could do anything they wanted."*

Roy Crain was the forceful tenor voice of the Soul Stirrers and the number two man of the group, but he was no substitute for the genius of R. H. Harris. Crain had spotted the still teenage Cooke singing with the Highway QCs and judged him to be the perfect replacement. Not that he was anything truly exceptional as a singer, but his boyish good looks and lean build matched the mood of the moment. When they showed up in Los Angeles in 1951 to cut a new album, Specialty Records boss Art Rupe wasn't too pleased. *"I said, where's Harris? They said, well he's gone and we want you to give Sam here a try. I thought he looked just a little kid but I reluctantly agreed rather than lose the whole session."* For Sam it was the main chance, fronting the premier gospel group of the time and still not yet come of age. Cooke and the Soul Stirrers were almost permanently on the road through the US, Canada and Mexico and Sam spent a glorious six year apprenticeship with them. *"I had a wonderful time, a wonderful life"*, he recalled later. *"I was doing the thing I liked best and getting paid for it. The fifty dollars or so a week I got at the beginning seemed like a fortune. I was just a teenager then. Later I earned more and more money until my salary more than tripled. It was one church after another on the one-nighter trail, and at that age, who cares about inconvenience?"*

Sam Cooke at first settled for a poor imitation of Harris but gradually evolved his own way with a song. *"Sam was a great thinker,"* said Harris, magnanimous in retreat. *"He was a singer who could stand and within the process of just singing, create without throwing the background off. I taught him that."* His first recordings with the Soul Stirrers for Specialty included Thomas Dorsey's *Peace In The Valley* and Roy Crain's song *I'm Gonna Build On That Shore*. Even at that early stage it's clear that the Cooke voice was shaping up as an exceptional asset and within a year or two the group was selling out everywhere they played. Jesse Farley remembered Sam's emergence as a youth idol:

> *"In the old days, young people took seats six rows from the back, the old folks stayed up front. When Sam came on the scene, it reversed itself. The young people took over... They started this pattern of standing up when the lead singers start bearing down."*

Finally, it all became too much of a commercial prospect for the gospel world to contain. During a Los Angeles appearance by the Soul Stirrers, Sam was quietly approached by the Specialty Records A & R man, Robert (Bumps) Blackwell, an old-time musician and arranger who formerly worked for Billy Eckstine, Earl Hines, Benny Carter and others.

> *"Bumps told me I ought to switch to the pop field,"* said Sam later. *"He said I had the voice, the confi-*

YOU'D BETTER RUN ON

dence and the equipment to work as a single, and that I ought to give it a try. Frankly, the pop field hadn't much attraction for me up until then. I was happy enough on the gospel trail and making myself a nice living. I liked the people I was working with and I was learning more and more about show-business every day. But the more I thought about the pop field the more interesting it became. Bumps, of course, had a good deal of influence. He was constantly prodding me to make the change whenever he got the chance. Then there were a lot of things I wanted to do. I wanted to do things for my family, and I wanted nice things of my own. Making a living was good enough, but what's wrong with doing better than that?"

Sam Cooke took the bait, quit the Soul Stirrers and studied the pop market. He listened to all the records, read all the trade papers and rehearsed with Blackwell. He even went to drama school for a while, but he wasn't entirely convinced that he was doing the right thing and his first secular record in 1957, *Lovable/Forever*, was issued under the pseudonym Dale Cook as if to hedge his bets. This fooled no-one and the record sold only modestly. The second was under his own name but *I'll Come Running Back To You* didn't do much better, prompting second thoughts all round.

Then Sam's brother, L. C. Cooke came up with *You Send Me* which they recorded for Specialty the same year. *"We had a lot of help on the session,"* Sam remembered. *"Bumps conducted the orchestra and S. R. Crain, my old mentor with the Soul Stirrers, helped on the arrangement. It was he who taught me to use my voice the way I do; the 'Oh, oh, oh' gimmick, which is now becoming so popular."*

Ironically, Art Rupe and Specialty rejected the song which subsequently went to No.1 and sold two and a half million copies. The company who picked up the recording was Bob Keene's own west coast Keene Records, with whom he stayed for nine chart entries including the classic *Only Sixteen*. The rest is soul history. Cooke took his place as the greatest of all black male singers in commercial music, fawned upon by the press, idolised by women for his charm and looks, revered by the rising generation of young gospel singers who would soon themselves dominate the pop market. He was the very first true superstar of soul but he was forever looking over his shoulder at the church he'd left behind. *"In those days, everybody who sang gospel believed that if you switched over to popular music, something bad would happen to you,"* said Sam's old guitarist Bobby Womack (himself an ex-gospel singer and now a bona-fide soul star in his own right). *"I grew up believing all that and I was afraid to make the change. See the gospel world used to be a lot more sacred than it is now."*

Even though Sam was now making the kind of money in a week that he'd have made in a year with the Soul Stirrers, he was continually drawn back to gospel, as if guilty of deserting it. When he formed his own record label SAR, he recorded the Stirrers and Harris's new group, the Paraders and he gave both Womack and the young Billy Preston their first starts. He even considered returning to gospel completely at one point in the early 1960s, but when he appeared at the Soul Stirrers anniversary in Chicago, the church put on its hardest and most unforgiving face. All the past group members were in attendance at the program and old Pop Harris himself was the master of ceremonies.

"While the Soul Stirrers were on stage, they called Sam up. I was the MC but I didn't know anything about it. Somehow when Sam hit the stage, the crowd went dead and stayed dead till Jimmy Outler and Paul Foster came back. Folks were hollering, 'Get that blues singer down. Get that no good so-and-so

down. This is a Christian programme.' And it pierced me to my heart, it shamed me how he was rejected by the home people. He walked off stage, tearin'. He was hurt badly."

Bobby Womack was even rejected by his own parents for leaving gospel.

"Our parents put us out of the house when we started singing pop music. My father said 'you will not bring the devil in here! If you gonna aim his pistol, I want him to know who to shoot.' In his last years he finally began to accept what I've done with my life. I told him, 'Dad, I just want you to see I'm the same guy. I coulda sung gospel to make you happy, but when you died we wouldn't have had the money to bury you."

Sam Cooke was shot dead in a Los Angeles motel on December 10th 1964. The woman who shot him alleged rape; Cooke's manager said he'd simply stumbled into the wrong room by mistake. Other stories claim it was a mafia killing. Whatever the truth, one of the finest soul voices - in or out of the church - had been silenced.

'At the Mt. Sinai Baptist Church in Los Angeles, a crowd of 5,000 persons, some of whom arrived five hours before the scheduled last rites, over-ran facilities designed to accommodate 1,500. In an emotion-packed atmosphere, super-charged by the singing of Lou Rawls, Bobby Blue Bland and Arthur Lee Simpkins, women fainted, tears rolled down men's cheeks and onlookers shouted. Gospel singer Bessie Griffin, who was to appear on the funeral program, became so grief stricken she had to be carried off. Blues singer Ray Charles stepped in from the audience to sing and play Angels Keep Watching Over Me. Outside some- one started a fistfight, and people paid freelance photographers to take pictures of them on the scene of Sam Cooke's funeral posing with a celebrity. One photographer was banished from the funeral parlour after he snapped pictures of Sam Cooke's casket, then peddled them outside for 25 cents apiece. Both in Chicago and Los Angeles, crowds crushed against the doors of the churches and around the cars so much that it took a flying wedge of security guards to get the family in and out. It was 40 minutes after the West Coast services ended before the two hundred-car cortege could set off to Forest Lawn Cemetery in Glendale where the singer was finally buried. Whatever the reasons for the crowds - genuine love or mere curiosity - they indicated thousands of persons' concern for facts about Sam Cooke's life and death.'

Ebony Magazine, February 1965

By consensus, Sam Cooke's very best work was with the Soul Stirrers. While the world remembers him for songs like *Twistin' The Night Away* and *Cupid* and *Having A Party*, surely his real magic is enshrined in all the exquisite Specialty sides he cut with the Soul Stirrers. Nothing he ever did in pop can compare with the searing beauty of *Wonderful* or the urgent narrative of *Touch The Hem Of His Garment* or the falsetto masterpiece *Jesus Wash Away My Troubles*.

Amid all the relative trivia he later came to record, perhaps only one song rises to the majesty of these gospel gems. Issued the year of his death, Sam's own song *A Change Is Gonna Come* is a modern soul clas- sic. The tune is pure gospel hymn, the lyrics are all hope. Contributing a soaring vocal performance that goes right back to R. H. Harris, Cooke evokes the mood of pilgrimage - both political and spiritual - that is

Photo: Cliff White.

Gospel's crossover superstars in the making:
Aretha Franklin and Sam Cooke contemplate their future.

African-America at its best:

'I was born by the river, in a little tent
And oh, just like the river, I been running ever since.
It's been a long time coming, but I know
A change is gonna come!'

The change, for **Aretha Franklin**, came when she was eighteen. Cooke was a close friend of the Franklin family and if he could make it in commercial music, why shouldn't she? After all, everyone said she could sing as good as Sam - some even reckoned she was better - and as Sam himself said, *"I'm making good money, and the devil ain't got me. I ain't left gospel."*

Aretha Franklin epitomises church-rooted soul singing. Neither James Brown nor Ray Charles - who along with Sam Cooke are always cited as the progenitors of soul - carry the same degree of gospel power over into their music. Aretha is altogether more deeply embedded in the gospel mystique, more so even than some of the great gospel names themselves.

It issues from the Franklin family background rather from any particular group experience like Cooke. Though Aretha made a handful of recordings as a gospel singer, she was never a household name in the way that Sam was. In fact, in many ways she is overshadowed as a gospel performer by her father, Rev Charles L. Franklin, who pastored Detroit's 4,500 member New Bethel Baptist Church. He recorded more than seventy albums of his sermons, which all sell heavily even today; for two decades he was one of the most famous of the gospel preachers, commanding thousands of dollars per appearance. At New Bethel, Rev Franklin would preach so hard that they had two white-uniformed nurses standing permanently by, to revive any overcome parishioners!

Rev C. L. Franklin may not have been a member of the Baptist Ministers Conference, but he could boast a Cadillac, diamond stick-pins and alligator skin shoes - all testifying to an eminently successful pastorate. In 1967 the Federal Government took a direct interest in the level of his success and fined him $25,000 for tax evasion. This is all a long way removed from St Francis of Assisi, but the Franklin sermons have an extraordinary power nonetheless, throwing echoes back through the sermons of Rev Gates and Rev McGhee to Franklin's own roots in the country churches of Mississippi. After short pastorates in Memphis and Buffalo, he moved into Detroit and set up home on the fringes of the city's East Side ghetto. The Franklin house was large, ramshackle and tree-shaded with a neatly kept lawn and Aretha grew up there, alongside many other kids who would eventually become huge stars - Diana Ross, Smokey Robinson and all the Four Tops to name but a few.

Half a block away, all the pursuits of the ghetto were in full swing. *"The people that you saw who had any measure of success were the pimp and the hustler, the numbers man and the dope man,"* recalls Aretha's older brother Cecil. It wasn't a happy childhood for Aretha, despite the fame and fortune of her father. Her mother deserted the family when she was six and died four years later, traumatic events that she never really got over. *"After her mama died,"* said Mahalia Jackson, *"the whole family wanted for love."* Franklin's long-time friends were the Clara Ward Singers and two of them - Frances Steadman and Marion Williams - stepped in to comfort Aretha and *"show her how to take care of herself."*

The Wards - Gertrude and Clara - were always in the house, so were Mahalia and Sam Cooke and James Cleveland. Any excuse for singing the good old gospel songs was taken up and Aretha would often sit in the corner and watch as the shouting, clapping and moaning went on all through the night. When one of her aunts died, she became mesmerised at the funeral as Clara Ward shouted herself into a trance on the old Dorsey song *Peace In The Valley*. In her fervour, Clara tore off her hat and hurled it to the ground. *"That,"* says Aretha, *"was when I wanted to become a singer."*

She was just twelve then and her first attempts at public performance were in New Bethel, mimicking all the mannerisms of Clara Ward. The church went wild over her from the very start; after her first solo, Franklin Snr was mobbed by his parishioners, telling him *"Oh, that child can sure enough sing!"*

Within two years, Aretha was a featured performer with the Franklin gospel caravan, an evangelistic team who toured endlessly by car - except for Rev Franklin himself, who chose to save his strength and travel by plane. The experience of the road encouraged her performing skills, but it also aged her prematurely. Cecil Franklin remembers it: *"Driving eight or ten hours trying to make a gig, and being hungry and passing restaurants all along the road, and having to go off the highway into some little city to find a place to eat because you're black - that had its effect."* In later years, Aretha would say only half-jokingly, *"I might be just 26 but I'm an old woman in disguise - 26 going on 65."*

By the time she was eighteen, Sam Cooke was hitting with pop records and Aretha's generation of young church singers were listening intently. One close friend was the young Jackie Verdell who'd been singing leads with the famous Davis Sisters, and the two girls decided to try out the commercial field that same year. For years it was touch and go who'd make it first. In fact it looked at first as if Jackie would be the most assured probability - her voice was the equal of Aretha's and she had a confidence in front of club audiences that Aretha lacked. *"I was afraid,"* said Aretha, *"I sang to the floor a lot."* Despite the commercial clout of a Columbia Records contract, nothing happened for Aretha Franklin until years later when she switched to Atlantic Records, dismissing her Columbia material by saying *"It really wasn't me."* Jerry Wexler was the producer at Atlantic and was shrewd enough to spot what was missing from the jazzy froth she'd been given to work with. *"I took her back to church,"* he said, *"sat her down at the piano, let her be herself."* To that he added the toughest R&B backing that Memphis could offer and the result was some of the very best music that has ever emerged from the soul factories of the 1960s. The first to take off was *I Never Loved A Man The Way I Loved You*; it sold a million copies in a matter of weeks. *"It had looked for the longest time like I would never have a gold record,"* said Aretha when she got the news, *"I wanted one so bad."*

The subsequent stream of immaculate soul hits followed the same formula of gospel stylings matched to R&B, and the Baptist preacher's daughter became the undisputed Queen of Soul. The public face of Aretha Franklin was of a woman in her element, at the very peak of her creative power, supremely successful as a commercial artist, a model for any young church singer with career ambition. They weren't to know the personal agonies and remorse she was suffering away from the stage lights. Her marriage to a Detroit street-hustler had been a disastrous mistake, the more so since Ted White had also taken over the management of her career. In 1967 there was a much publicised incident when White's private brutality spilled over into public and he openly beat her up in the foyer of Atlanta's Regency Hyatt House Hotel.

Aretha Franklin sings at Mahalia Jackson's funeral (L).
Centre: Aretha under the watchful eye of Daddy C. L. Franklin.

Top: Rev C. L. Franklin with his young daughter Aretha.
Below: C. L. Franklin preaching at New Bethel Baptist Church, Detroit.

Nor was it the only such incident, prompting Mahalia Jackson to comment tersely, *"I don't think she's happy. I think somebody else is making her sing the blues."*

When she visited Europe that same year she was still intensely neurotic - 'peeping out from behind her self-imposed curtain,' wrote Leonard Feather in the Melody Maker. On stage at London's Hammersmith Odeon though, she opened up sufficiently to turn the audience inside out, especially when seated alone at the piano for songs like *Dr Feelgood*. Even coasting on a blues tune, Aretha is more emotion than most people can handle.

Within two years, her isolation was virtually complete. On a David Frost British TV show in November 1970, she was monosyllabic and defensive until they sat her at the piano. She chose to sing *Precious Lord*, defying show-business conventions by calling to camera 'I'm strong in my religion. I wish other people knew Him like I do.' Val Wilmer, writing in Down Beat, found her to be 'plagued with a feeling of insecurity. She seems to come to life only on the stage.' And in the Observer Sunday newspaper, Tony Palmer commented that Aretha 'has become impenetrable, even to her friends.'

This wasn't the petulance of a prima donna's ego. At the heart of her trouble lay the realisation that she wasn't simply a great voice who happened to learn her stuff singing for the Lord. She was a gospel singer through and through and the commercial music business was anathema to her soul. Her gospel family were the only ones who properly understood this and she confided her anguish only to them. She went eventually to Mahalia Jackson, as a daughter to her spiritual mother, and told her, *"I'm gonna make a gospel record and tell Jesus I cannot bear these burdens alone."*

For some reason, Aretha had never drawn the same sort of extreme censure from the church that other deserters had. Perhaps it was C. L. Franklin's status that inhibited the critics or perhaps it was because they sensed that she had never really left them. Aretha was like an icon that had been borrowed for an exhibition and whose owners were patiently expecting its return. The demons that she wrestled with were very private but the battle for her soul was public enough. *"I'm looking for Aretha to come back one of these days,"* said a close church friend, *"She won't be happy till she does."*

Finally, she did it. In January 1972, James Cleveland assembled his Southern California Community Choir and Atlantic set up their mobile recording unit in the new Temple Missionary Baptist Church in Los Angeles. Aretha was back home in front of an ecstatic congregation and she turned the whole building out. Not since her first recordings in New Bethel had Aretha hit this level of spiritual intensity and, over a two day period, she improvised on the hymns and gospel tunes closest to her heart: the Clara Ward classic *How I Got Over* (Clara was in the congregation with mother Gertrude, who moaned away in the background), Inez Andrews' song *Mary Don't You Weep* and of course Dorsey's *Precious Lord*. It's one of the oldest of spirituals - *Amazing Grace* - that inspired her to the greatest heights however, and she took ten and a half minutes to practice her extraordinary art to the utmost limit. This was the Queen of Soul's finest moment and she drew on all her prodigious vocal powers to wring every drop of pathos and drama out of the hymn. Even on record, it is almost unbearable in its extremity and it can still move the hardest heart to tears. If anyone should doubt Aretha's true musical calling, they should be placed alone in front of an efficient sound system and made to experience the full atmosphere of this event. Even at second-hand, the home-coming of Aretha Franklin is the ultimate gospel encounter.

As the entranced choir and congregation attempted to recompose themselves, James Cleveland brought Rev C. L. Franklin up to address them. *"This"*, he said as they dabbed their eyes and fanned their brows, *"Took me all the way back to the living room at home, when she was six or seven years of age. I saw you crying and I saw you respond, but I was ready to bust wide open. You talk about being moved - well, not only because Aretha is my daughter ... Aretha's just a stone singer. If you wanna know the truth,"* he declared with bursting pride, *"She has never left the church!"*

It should have been a happy ending, but nothing's quite that simple it seems. Just one month later, the great Mahalia Jackson's heart gave out and Aretha went to the funeral of one of her closest and wisest friends, singing *Precious Lord* over mother Halie's body just as the gospel matriarch had sung it over the body of Martin Luther King. If the constraints of the music industry hadn't been so overpowering, then she might have picked up Mahalia's crown at that point and kissed the world goodbye. As it was, she returned to an increasingly lack-lustre career in pop music and the church got by without her. The last time I saw her in 1982, she was such a sad caricature of her former glory, lumbering half-heartedly through her least demanding pop hits, grossly underselling a bitterly disappointed audience. I can't really believe that it's by free choice that she wastes herself in this way, to the extent that she even hires a third-rate session tambourine player so lacking in feel that she must provide him with sheet music. More than anything else in her performance, this was the most poignant symbol of gospel's corruption by commercial ethics.

When C. L. Franklin sank into a coma after a shooting incident, Aretha drew back to nurse him and share in his silent isolation. After years of devoted seclusion she consented to break her vigil and take the lead in *'Sing, Mahalia, Sing'*. Preparing to open in Detroit in the summer of 1984, the fates once again intervened in her life and daddy C.L. slipped from his coma over into glory. Mahalia's story should perhaps have been Aretha's own but she never got to play it for real and now was unable even to play it as make-believe.

Three years later and still mourning the loss of her father, she went back to New Bethel Baptist Church in Detroit and recorded her second gospel album (third if you count the recordings she made for Battle as a teenager). 'One Lord, One Faith, One Baptism' is typical of Aretha's uncompromising approach to gospel music and she gathered around her this time her family and friends - Rev Jesse Jackson, Mavis Staples, Joe Ligon and Minister Thomas Whitfield. Whitfield was the new gospel production maestro who'd just cut Vanessa Bell Armstrong's great *Peace Be Still* album and, had Aretha allowed him full reign to produce this in similar fashion, it too might have reached the heights of *Amazing Grace*. As it is and despite Brewster's great *Surely God Is Able*, the record fails to completely fulfil its collective promise.

Neither Aretha nor Sam Cooke were the first to market their soul. For many people, Ray Charles is the greatest gospel singer who never was. Arguably, he was the first major artist to take the essential gospel sounds and fashion them into a saleable commodity. Maybe because he was never a gospel singer in the first place, Brother Ray has never had the same kind of traumatic relationship with the church that Sam and Aretha had. Ray had no compunction about taking the moans of the saints and the cries of Archie Brownlee, underpinning them with down-home gospel piano and calling it soul. He is the great paradox of African-American music - the father of the soul movement, brought up in the Baptist faith, who has studiously avoided any direct gospel references, while embracing every other genre from jazz to country and western. *"All music is related,"* he told Gary Kramer, *"A gospel music background is important to a jazz musician for it draws out feeling. What you speak of as soul in jazz is soul in gospel music. The important thing in jazz is to feel your music, but really feel it and believe it - the way a gospel singer like Mahalia Jackson obviously feels and believes the music she is singing, with her whole body and soul."*

Ray is almost on the defensive about gospel music and he'll usually try to change the subject, as if embarrassed about the use he's made of it. It's not generally known for instance that Ray has a huge collection of gospel records, mostly duplicated onto tape and carried round with him. Alex Bradford, the hard shouting gospel professor from Alabama, was a big influence on him; *"Ray Charles told me I was his ideal as a gospel singer, and if I ever wanted to send him a song, all I'd have to do is announce my name and he'd give it first preference."*

Charles' predilection for a good gospel song provided him with some of his biggest hits. *What'd I Say, Hallelujah, I Just Love Her So* and *This Little Girl of Mine* are all fairly direct parodies (the latter being the most blatant steal from Clara Ward's *This Little Light of Mine*) but his plagiarism extends even to the more obscure material - in *Lonely Avenue* he does a note-for-note copy of *How Jesus Died* by Jess Whitaker of the Pilgrim Travellers. Big Bill Broonzy was scathing of his method: *"He's got the blues, he's crying sanctified. He's mixing the blues with the spirituals. I know that's wrong ... he should be singing in a church."*

For all this, Ray Charles must still be reckoned as a musical genius. We can only speculate what he might have been capable of had he sung gospel, but his performances (particularly his live performances) of heart-tearing songs like *A Fool For You* are among some of the most moving moments in soul music. At the Newport Festival in 1973, on the same bill as Aretha Franklin and the Staple Singers, he held a vast crowd spell-bound with *Just A Man* - solo at the piano with his own song of the most profound lyrical beauty. Outside of gospel, it is one of the few recordings that can be counted as an ultimate artistic statement; and if that sounds like pretension then it's a necessary inadequacy in the face of such expressive music.

Brother Ray opened the door to show-business for ambitious young gospel singers and in so doing he fathered the soul music movement. LaVern Baker and Dinah Washington married church and pop music before he did, but he was the catalyst for its final emergence as soul. As Nesuhi Ertegun says, *"Ray wasn't the first to do this, combine gospel and blues. He is the best of a long tradition - there were people singing this way twenty years ago. But Ray was able to bring so much of his own to it."* A lot of young gospel singers went through the door that Ray Charles had opened. Apart from Sam Cooke and Aretha, Lou Rawls came out of the Pilgrim Travellers, Wilson Pickett left the Violinaires, the Fairfield Four said goodbye to Roscoe Robinson and Joe Henderson, David Ruffin moved on from the Dixie Nightingales and the Soul Stirrers produced another graduate in the person of Johnnie Taylor. Don Robey, boss of Duke-Peacock Records, took Joe Hinton from his lead position with the Spirit of Memphis with the idea of making 'another Sam Cooke' out of him. Clearly, not all who defected found their fame and fortune.

The Drinkard Singers of New Jersey were one of the more successful 'academies' of soul, having launched the singing careers of no less than four popular artists - Judy Clay, Cissy Houston and sisters Dee Dee and

Dionne Warwick. Contrary to popular myth, Dionne never actually recorded with the Drinkard Singers but, as she told me, *"You might say I cut my teeth on this music ... coming from a gospel singing family, that was the music and teachings I grew up with. It was, and it still is, the happiest sounding and feeling music that I know. They were the best singers I ever heard - I'm proud to be part of that family."*

And what a family for Cissy Houston's little girl to grow up in. Whitney Houston has almost picked up where Aretha left off and, though not yet in the same league as a singer, has refined the process of church-influenced soul singing, taking it to undreamed-of heights. Whitney has yet to record a full-fledged gospel album but she regularly includes uncompromising songs like *Yes Jesus Loves Me* in her stage set, much as Patti La Belle and other high profile Christian entertainers do. She is close friends with a number of contemporary gospel artists like BeBe and CeCe Winans (guesting on their recording of *Hold Up The Light*) and it is an intriguing prospect to think what she may one day be capable of in gospel music. We might not have long to wait - she has promised Arista Records that a gospel album is an absolute priority.

While it has become commonplace for individual singers to leave gospel groups and cross over to pop, it is much rarer to find whole groups crossing over to the secular field and even rarer for them to achieve anything at all by it. In the early 1950s the Selah Jubilee Singers, who had given twenty-five years to gospel quartet singing, were persuaded to switch to pop by Bess Berman of Apollo Records and they ended up ignominiously as The Larks. The long established New Orleans Humming Four heeded the call of the Imperial Record company and became The Hawks. Another New Orleans quartet, the Delta Southernaires, were marginally more successful in rock 'n' roll as The Spiders. This is not exactly a 'Hall of Fame'.

One of the very few groups to have enjoyed real success in both gospel and pop is the Staple Singers. As a family group, the Staples can look back over a career spanning forty six years, dividing almost exactly into two parts. In 1950, Roebuck Staples strapped on his $60 pawnshop guitar and presented three of his children to the Mount Zion Baptist church in Chicago where his brother Rev Chester Staples was pastor. Cleotha, Pervis and Mavis sang spirituals over the bluesy chords of Pops' guitar and the congregation, in their white shirts, slicked hair and fancy clothes started crying and wouldn't stop. There's something in the way the Staple Singers harmonised back then that immediately evoked memories of the old South for the hardened city exiles and the family were soon in great demand around the Chicago churches.

Roebuck of course, was one of the exiles himself. He was born in 1915 in Winona, Mississippi and started out learning the blues guitar styles of Big Bill Broonzy and Barbecue Bob while working in the plantations. He got converted when he was 15, started singing in the Baptist Church and joined up with local group the Golden Trumpets a year later. For a couple of years he toured with them round the Mississippi churches but the Depression was destroying the cotton industry, and he and his wife Oceola and their two children added themselves to the long trek northwards in search of work. Like so many others, they settled in Chicago and Roebuck took up with another gospel group, the Trumpet Jubilees. The explosion of new gospel sounds was happening in Chicago at exactly the same time and all the excitement generated by Thomas Dorsey and Sallie Martin over at Pilgrim Baptist Church, had a profound influence on the young Roebuck. He had a family to look out for though and he worked long hours in the steel-mill, the docks, the construction site and the car wash, bringing them all safely through the Depression and the war years.

While Yvonne and Mavis were still at school, the family group were called to the studios of United Records in 1953 where they cut about eight sides. United only issued two of them - *Sit Down Servant* (issued as *Won't You Sit Down*) and *It Rained Children*, selling the rest off later to the Sharp and Gospel labels. *Sit Down Servant* was just another traditional spiritual on a two-bit label and it didn't set the world on fire. "It sold about 200, that first thing," said Roebuck.

> "They heard us - a lady from the record company - and liked us, so we recorded. But the man who owned the company, he wanted us to do rock 'n' roll ... we wanted no part of rock 'n' roll. So he held us for two years on contract with that one record. When his contract was up, Vee Jay asked us to come and do a record, so we did and that record sold 1,000. The first Vee Jay record we made was *If I Could Hear My Mother Pray Again* and as it sold 1,000 I thought Vee Jay was disappointed with us, so we were ready to quit. But Vee Jay said 'No, no, when will you be ready to go into the studio?' And I said, 'I'm ready to go in now', so we went in and we made *Uncloudy Day* and it sold like rock 'n' roll!"

Uncloudy Day isn't by any stretch of the imagination the stuff of a conventional smash hit, but it is undoubtedly one of gospel's masterpieces. A ponderous blues hymn, it ushered in the two dominant features of Staples' music - the heavily tremeloed, economic beauty of Roebuck's guitar and the awesome, sensual voice of Mavis Staples. Their years with Vee Jay produced their greatest artistic triumphs - 30-40 tracks that are quite unlike anything else in gospel music. They are instantly recognisable from the thousands of groups of the time, not simply by their sound but by the subtle pleadings of their performance.

Roebuck is one of the most under-rated of guitarists, possibly because he is a master of the understatement, using an absolute economy of notes, sometimes almost as if he can't bear to actually touch the strings. Mavis, on the other hand, is one of the most moving of all African-American singers. Particularly on these early recordings, her breathy exhortation and searing entreaties are the embodiment of all the traditions of gospel and she is the consummate communicator on stage. On the occasions I've heard her in person, she seems to be able to summon up super-human qualities from the far reaches of her soul, leaving her audience breathless and dumbstruck. Even during the later programmes when much of the time they sounded like a disco outfit, Mavis will pick out a slow spiritual and stalk up and down the stage with her arms jacking downwards, piling on the emotive fervour until those standing open-mouthed beneath her can't take it any more. Then she'll pause and savour the moment, shaking with exhaustion, until she gets her breath back. And just when they think she's coming back down, she'll start in again and force them up and over the limit.

There was always a degree of speculation about whether the Staple singers would cross-over. One of the last recordings they did for Vee Jay was a version of the Tindley hymn *Stand By Me* which featured Mavis at her most impassioned and vibrant best. Had it been secularised and given a lush backing it would have halved the effect but doubled the sales potential. (Leiber and Stoller saw the chance and did just that for Ben E. King). Another of the Staples' 1958 recordings *This May Be The Last Time* was stolen by the Rolling Stones and turned into big money.

When they did finally make moves in a commercial direction, it wasn't at first into soul music but into folk. Bob Dylan went around for years eulogising over the group and especially over the voice of Mavis

Photos: Bill Greensmith/Library
of Congress.

Top: The Staple Singers of Chicago, Illinois.
Below: A typical storefront church, Chicago, c.1944.

Photo: Val Wilmer.

Rev Pearly Brown, Macon, Georgia, 1973.

Staples and they eventually signed to Riverside Records where they did a series of tepid 'folk-gospel' albums. The white folk music fans loved them, but Pops wasn't too happy:

> "Riverside really tried to put us in a folk bag so we could be more commercial and we could sell records, but we still didn't quite make it with them. When it didn't work we tried Columbia. Our first producer there, Billy Sherill, couldn't find us either so they brought in Larry Williams."

Their material till then had been strictly devotional - either traditional spirituals or Roebuck's own gospel tunes. In 1967 they were persuaded to secularise the message - take out any direct references to God or Jesus, and substitute vague concepts of love and understanding. That way the label got themselves a saleable commodity and the Staples were able to convince themselves that they hadn't sold out. The first of the Larry Williams productions was *Why Am I Treated So Bad* and it proved the label's point by entering the Hot 100. A year later they switched to Stax, where Al Bell began to produce the kind of soul hits that finally took them to international acclaim. *Heavy Makes You Happy* was the first to go really high in the charts and Mavis was both relieved and delighted. *"We knew Al had the sound we were looking for. We started doing much bigger shows, rock concerts. We just got bigger and bigger. Respect Yourself earned us a gold disc of course. It started with the kids, you know they had little slogans saying Respect Yourself which they'd attach on the backs of their shirts and stuff."*

Fame bought them the respect they deserved from the rest of the world but they were fast losing it from the church. Author of *The Gospel Sound* Tony Heilbut described how deeply their rejection was felt:

> "On Thanksgiving Day 1969, they made a rare gospel appearance in Philadelphia, where Mavis' latest ballad was a smash hit. They went back to the same routine that had sustained them for years; the Staples are probably the only gospel group who still feature the songs they sang in 1956. Mavis shook hands on Help Me Jesus and groaned with suffering on Tell Heaven I'm Coming Home One Day. Philadelphia remained very still. The girls walked off stage shyly and obviously hurt. But Roebuck wouldn't give up. 'Listen church, you have to look out for yourself,' he said strumming the guitar. 'Don't nobody want to go to heaven more than I do, children, but we got to live down here too.' The message was clear, but no 'amens' resounded. Finally Roebuck brought Mavis back to sing Precious Lord. I've seldom seen her work harder. She was all over the audience, crying, roaring, running. Four ladies screamed, the least such effort deserved, but the rest of the church remained very still. The applause was barely polite as Cleotha led the entranced Mavis out."

Mavis always defends the move into commercialism, but she doesn't come across with any great conviction. *"You know since we become 'stars', whatever that is, it's been pretty hectic and everything moves kinda fast. Be What You are, I'll Take You There, If You're Ready, Come Go With Me - our records are kinda funky but we still do message songs. But we had to move with the times. Now we try to get our message across to a bigger audience, that's all. I don't think the message in our lyrics has changed since those times. Sure, the beat's got harder, but the message is the same."*

Pops Staples, now in his eighties, is currently enjoying a renaissance on the blues concert circuit but Mavis is seemingly never to receive her due recognition, despite the patronage of super-stars like Prince.

These days it's almost obligatory for famous soul stars to allude to a gospel background - mostly real but occasionally imagined. It does a grave disservice though to gospel music, to conclude that it functions merely as a training ground for promising soul singers. There are dozens of singers who choose to remain exclusively in gospel, who stand head and shoulders in every way over the big names of soul - Shun Pace Rhodes, Yolanda Adams, Karen Clark, Daryl Coley and Tramaine Hawkins are just a few from the current spiritual crop. And for every one who crossed over and made it big, there are hundreds who crossed over and didn't. Whereas Aretha Franklin lives in fabulous, if troubled, luxury - Jackie Verdell, who made the same move at the same time, made nothing at all and returned to singing gospel, facing a faintly suspicious audience.

It's difficult to escape the conclusion that the soul music industry has attempted to colonise the church for its own financial gain. That some have been tempted by its offers of glittering reward is hardly surprising. What is more surprising is that so many of the best gospel singers remained and resisted the corruption of African-American church music. Maybe with good justification they can say, 'What shall it profit a man if he gain the whole world and lose his own soul.'

Perhaps that was the conclusion Al Green came to. Like thousands of others he joined the one-way traffic out of the church and into the soul limelight. Then, right at the very peak of his commercial career when he was quite the biggest soul star of the 1970s, he did the most extraordinary thing and quit - to become minister of the Full Gospel Tabernacle on Hale Rd in Memphis. It was the most sensational turn-around and it had a huge impact on modern gospel music. Not so much musically, though he has forced some important changes, more a kind of psychological boost for gospel morale. Al Green, the man they called The Last Soul Singer in America, the voice that stirred a million hearts, the mentor of countless lesser singers, had finally decided that there was more to life than 'scooby-dooby-doo' and had packed up shop and gone on home to Jesus, just like the prodigal son.

He's not the first to have done it. Solomon Burke went from child preacher to soul star and back again and Little Richard's done the trip a few times, but the conversion of Al Green was a massive propaganda coup for gospel music. When he stood up in the pulpit and declared *"He took the rock 'n' roll and the twisting the night away from me, and gave me a new song, a song the angels can sing, and I want you to know his name is Jesus"*, he was turning the tide of the last forty years ... all of his then lifetime.

Al Green grew up in Forrest City, Arkansas (an hour's drive from his current home) and got a staple diet of gospel music from his family. *"I was raised on it,"* he remembered. *"It was put into my cornbread. I ate it. My mother and my father, they were Baptists. We were raised in church, and we sang at home. I started when I was a little peewee. I was just raised on the sound of Sam Cooke and the Soul Stirrers and the whole trip; yeah, that was in the house."*

Al joined up with his brothers as a family gospel group, the Green Brothers, and got his first taste of performing as their tenor lead. Sam Cooke had just switched to pop and Al Green couldn't wait to join him. Clandestine visits to the local record store to catch up on Sam's new style were fuel to his fire but when father found out, he was exiled from the house. It's something that still hurts. If you ask him whether his family liked his pop records, he'll get very tight-lipped and mutter *"No. They were gospel folks. No."*

Green had moved up to Grand Rapids Michigan, where he scored a local hit with *Back Up Train* in 1967, but it took a few more years of struggle and business rip-offs before he finally got his big break with veteran producer and bandleader Willie Mitchell. Mitchell took him back down to Memphis and they recorded his first million seller in 1971, *I'm So Tired Of Being Alone*. Over the next five years he emerged as the brightest star in soul music, selling over thirty million records, picking up just about every award going and in every way taking over the throne vacated by the big 1960s names like Otis Redding, with classic singles ... *Let's Stay Together* and *Take Me To The River*.

The return of Al Green to his gospel roots didn't happen in a blinding flash, but was a gradual process that extended over a period of four or five years. There are conflicting accounts of what triggered the transformation, including the famous story that he was burned by hot grits thrown by a scorned lover, but he dismisses all this as fiction.

> *"I was born again in 1973,"* he says, *"Yeah, transfigured, transformed. It wasn't an incident that did it. No. People are silly when they write that. Nothing happened to bring me to Christ except coming into the knowledge of Christ and being transformed in mind and spirit on a particular morning. Like the old singers sing, 'There's one thing I know/That I've been born again'. Right. That's all I can speak about, that it has happened to me. I'm a gospel singer now, and when it happened to me, I was singing rock 'n' roll."*

And he carried on singing rock 'n' roll. Not until 1977 did he begin to put his faith on record, with the critically acclaimed *Belle* album, a mystical tribute to the indivisibility of sensual and spiritual love.

> *"That was the kick-off, the initial thrust-off, the saying that I'm going to do it. I'm going to follow that. If you are really genuine, why don't you go for the real treasure? Now I know all about the financial treasure and that whole trip, but I ain't worried about that. I'm talking about the real treasure, Jesus."*
> Another time he said of the Belle Album, *"The religious naturally goes with art because they're both so ancient. I think Belle was the kind of record it was because it channelled both - religion and rock 'n' roll - and it channelled them so well."*

His next record was *Truth & Time* and it took his pre-occupation with things spiritual to further lengths, but behind the scenes he was slowly being torn apart by all the demands being made on him. Not simply the excesses of super-stardom but all of that in fierce conflict with his growing Christian faith. The crunch came - literally - at what turned out to be his last concert as a pop singer. In Cincinnati, in September of 1979, Green fell twelve feet off the stage onto a flight case.

> *"I spent fifteen days in the hospital and I realised I was being disobedient to my calling. I was moving towards God, but I wasn't moving fast enough. The fall was God's way of saying I had to hurry up."*

Nowadays, Al Green has learned how to relax, even though he's still under pressure. How, I asked, did he cope with the vastly different demands he faces as a pastor? *"These days,"* he answered slowly, *"I have to divide my time between my singing and my church in Memphis and well, I do my best to rightly divide it. And I have to devote a sufficient amount of time to do a good job, which is kinda difficult sometimes. I preach every other Sunday in church and I do concerts and records when I can."*

Photo: Viv Broughton.

Rev Al Green.

Of his years as a soul hero, he confesses that it's mostly just a blur. *"The only thing I really remember is lights, plenty of lights, always lights, always psssh, pssh - singing songs and just lights. I don't remember which days, which nights - who came where in what car, I don't remember ... just like waking up off a dream - this flood of lights. People screaming, the Apollo Theatre, roses, this hustle and this bustle. So, so much going on."* but he doesn't reject it all out of hand as other converts might. *"No regrets,"* he says firmly, *"It was wonderful. It was bringing you to where you can understand what you're doing now."* And of his old hits he says, *"They're good songs that won't drive people to war."*

The reborn Al Green goes much further than that in his music. With a renewed purpose and vision, he's singing better than ever, though his records have been on the smaller gospel labels and consequently much harder to find. The first all gospel album for Myrrh came in 1980 (*The Lord Will Make A Way*) leading up through *Higher Plane* in 1981 to the peak of Green artistry that is *Precious Lord*. It won him a Grammy and at the award ceremony Al returned to face once again the cynical music business he'd spurned. He brought them all to their feet with a stunning live performance, as if to prove that now he was more of a soul singer, not less. Robert Hilburn of the LA Times wrote then that *"There's no question that he has the same potential to be one of the most successful artists ever in gospel music."*

He's the man who came full circle, the man who re-claimed soul music for the church but his earthy, insinuous way with a song and his occasional inclusion of those secular hits in concert, doesn't always go down well with the more traditional folks. Some have even walked out on him in church.

"Yeah, it's different from other gospel music," he concedes, *"But I think the message, the story is the same. Yeah, I believe so. You don't have to use the same format that has been used for the past fifty years. You can come up to the present day to deliver the same message and do it with a bit of class and quality."*

As a producer he brought the same sort of quality to the records of groups like the New York Community Choir and close associates like Laura Lee - who began in gospel as Della Reese's replacement in the Meditation Singers, went on to become the deepest and most radical of women soul singers, then teamed up with Al Green in Memphis after her own Christian conversion.

Al Green's supreme ability was always to move the listener, to touch the heart deeply with joy or sorrow, and none of these very special qualities had in any way diminished in the man. Rather, his unrivalled skill as a communicator harnessed to the new fire in his soul, conspired to produce a fresh spiritual music that was awesome in its power and beauty.

And who knows how many he inspired - throughout the 80s and into the 90s, other high-profile names in soul music began to return to the gospel fold - Helen Baylor, Candi Staton, Deniece Williams, Patti La Belle, Stephanie Mills and Jennifer Holliday have all now come home to gospel.

If Al Green was the great prodigal son of the gospel church, then these are the prodigal daughters and, hallelujah, they're right back where they belong. ❖

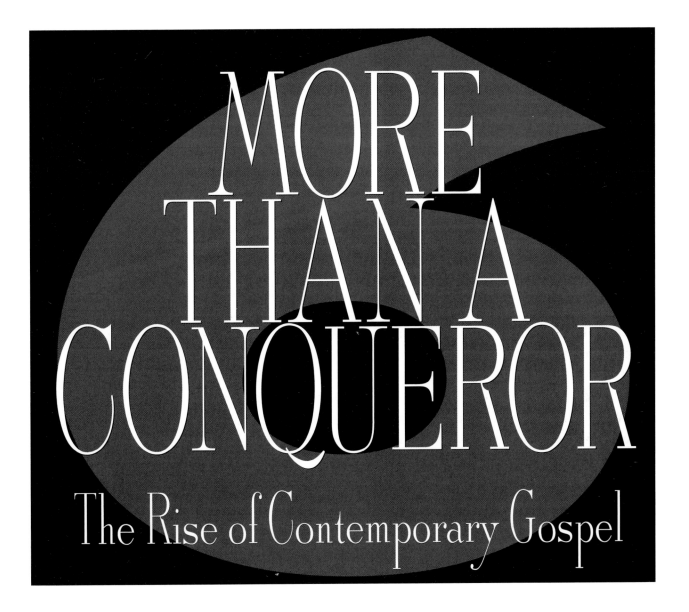

MORE THAN A CONQUEROR

The Rise of Contemporary Gospel

"For months now (and in the record business, months are decades), desperate music hustlers have been searching for the new groove ... Last week, with appropriate fanfare, they proclaimed they had found the sound: pop gospel. Waving contracts and recording tape, Columbia Records moved into a new Manhatten night club called the Sweet Chariot and began packaging such devotional songs as He's All Right for the popular market. 'It's the greatest new groove since rock 'n' roll', said Columbia A&R Director David Kapralik.
'In a month or two, it'll be all over the charts'."

Laughable predictions like this had uncanny parallels in the 80s and 90s, but this one, in fact, goes back to the mid-1960s, when *Time* magazine was reporting on the 'gospel night club' phenomenon that appeared in several American cities.

Joe Scandore was the New York entrepreneur behind the idea, inveigling the unfortunate Nat Lewis Singers from one of the largest Pentecostal churches on the East coast, and the Ellison family gospel group - the Golden Chords, to take part in his ill-conceived venture. The Chords were led by Lorraine Ellison (later to achieve brief but spectacular acclaim for her soul music classic *Stay With Me Baby*) who brought in the Philadelphia All Stars to become the Sweet Chariot Singers; Joe took over the lease on the Peppermint Lounge, turning the former campaign headquarters of the Twist into *The Sensational New Pop Gospel Night Club With 'Soul'*.

The Sweet Chariot opened in May 1963 and drew enormous crowds for an experience that was bizarre almost beyond belief. The club hostesses were clad in choir robes that reached only to the thigh, where they met opera length stockings. Attached to the back of the robe were two small angel wings and the ensemble was crowned with a wire halo. While the 'angels' served liquor, the singers crooned *What Do You Know About Jesus?* The smart money, as they say, went for it in a big way. Customers (including Barbra Streisand, Neil Sedaka and Diana Dors among hordes of other minor celebs and socialites) collected their tambourines at the door and relieved themselves in toilets labelled 'Brothers' and 'Sisters'. Kapralik hardly needed to point out that *"These people are not here for a religious catharsis, they are here for entertainment."*

It wasn't gospel music's most edifying moment.

Mercifully, the fad passed within a year but not before Columbia Records had milked three live albums out of the Sweet Chariot groups, all uniformly repellent - affectations of frenzy and parodies of African-American religious music. There's an unconscious irony in the cover photo of one album showing the singers holding tambourines clearly, but unconvincingly, marked 'Not For Sale'. Another album carries the barely less plausible claim that 'this album may well serve to mark a turning point in America's musical history; a time when gospel music, of and by itself, is reaching the wide audience it deserves.'

After that little episode it's surprising that gospel was able to command any audience at all, outside of the churches, and indeed six years passed before the music next reached the mass market. Then it was to be in the form of an old Baptist hymn re-arranged by a young Holiness pianist and singer from California - Edwin Hawkins.

In the meantime the church just got on with the business of being the church and gospel singers just got on with the business of spreading the gospel, perhaps even relieved that the secular record industry had once again failed them. Despite all the bribes and seductions of the music business, gospel has survived as the only remaining slice of African-American culture that is relatively inviolate. It's often discreetly suggested by some white people that this is a function of inverted prejudice - a black religious exclusivity - when it's simply the defence mechanisms of a culture under attack. Gospel singers aren't hostile to white people, only to the cultural presumptions and ambitions that they invariably bring with them.

Rev James Cleveland personified the cultural defender, resolutely defying every attempt to draw him into the mainstream of American entertainment:

> *"I will not perform for the white man for the purpose of financial profit ... I don't feel I can do much good in a club. I don't feel that the atmosphere is conducive, and I don't feel that the reason for bringing me there is the reason for which I'm singing. I feel that if they want religious music in the clubs, in the casinos*

where folks are ten feet away and drinking and gambling, then they should get white singers ... But they would not insult the intelligence of white singers by asking them to sing in a club."

Cleveland wasn't a political radical by any means, but he was an extremely astute and commanding figure-head for gospel music at its most uncompromising. Where others would twist and turn and accommodate the curious and usually insensitive outsiders, he acquired over many long years the right to demand accep-tance on his own terms and his own terms only. He was especially scathing about those who sought mere-ly a vicarious musical diversion in the gospel experience: *"You'll find that most white folks, when they do come to a Black concert, all they want to hear is your up-tempo stuff. They're not concerned about the message you're trying to give. They just want a funky beat, something they can clap their hands to, and they enjoy it because it's fun to them."*

Right up until his death in 1991, James Cleveland was the heavyweight champion of gospel music and inevitably he was dubbed 'The Godfather' by friends and enemies alike. He seems to have been everywhere and always in gospel music, his booming gravel voice on a hundred albums, his name linked to all the great names from the first to the last, his imposing barrel frame fronting dozens of choirs from East coast to West. His many gold albums, his countless production and publishing credits and his massive personal appearance fees all served to accord him superstar status in his Beverley Hills home, surrounded by all the trappings of success - a hundred suits, fifty pairs of shoes, a Persian lamb overcoat ('made by the best furrier in Chicago') and a veritable truckload of trophies and awards.

It wasn't always so for James. He was born slap bang into the Depression in Chicago and raised in the strict traditions of the gospel church. *"My folks being just plain everyday people, we couldn't afford a piano. So I used to practice each night right there on the window-sill. I took those wedges and crevices and made me black and white keys. And baby ... by the time I was in high school, I was some jazz pianist."*

Showing remarkable prescience, his first minister at Pilgrim Baptist Church was the grand old man him-self - Thomas A. Dorsey, so the young James Cleveland had the very best of training as a singer and pianist. His grandmother Annie used to carry him to the choir rehearsals. When I talked to him in 1985, he remembered Dorsey with great affection:

> *"Thomas was, like ... magic, you know. I would go to choir rehearsals with my grandmother and I'd be just electrified by him. He was just about the only exponent of gospel music in those days - he was teaching it and putting choirs together before anyone else."*

By the time he was sixteen, he was writing songs and selling them to the pioneer gospel singer and pub-lisher Roberta Martin at $40 a time. Two years later he cut his first records for the Apollo label as part of the Gospelaires - not the major quartet from Dayton, Ohio, but a short-lived spin off from the old Roberta Martin Singers.

The 1950s saw him in various guises, none especially satisfactory, but he spent time with the Caravans and featured on two of their big hits *The Solid Rock* and *What Kind Of Man*. Albertina Walker tells how she first met up with James:

"I needed a musician and happened to come in off the road. I ran over to Mahalia Jackson's house and James was there. I asked him if he wanted to play for the Caravans and that was that. The record company didn't want to record James though because they didn't think he could sing - they said he sounded like a frog! But I told the record company man that I wasn't going to record unless he recorded James!"

At the end of the decade, James began his famous association with choirs, working first with the Voices of Tabernacle from Detroit and taking them to national fame with a gospel ballad borrowed from Johnnie Taylor and the Soul Stirrers - *The Love Of God*. Discovering that James wasn't, in fact, under contract at that point, the sagacious Herman Lubinsky moved in and snapped him up for his Savoy label against some stiff competition. *"I didn't want to go with him because I wanted to go to Vee Jay which was a big successful company then."* Lubinsky out-manoeuvred Vee Jay though and the Cleveland signature inaugurated a recording partnership that endured to the very end.

His first choir album for Savoy was devised by Fred Mendelsohn, the new A&R man on the label and eventually the overall boss of Savoy. He set Cleveland up with the Angelic Choir of Nutley, New Jersey to make the album *Christ Is The Answer*.

"It was recorded under very tough circumstances. We were in the cellar of this very old church, before the Angelic Choir and Rev Lawrence Roberts rebuilt their church in the 1960s, and it was one of the most exciting afternoons I can remember. We were in the cellar, we ran the equipment down there. It wasn't of the best kind. In fact I think we recorded monaural. But we could hear the excitement mounting through the walls and floor when the choir was singing, and when James was singing, and especially when the choir was really getting the Spirit. That was very successful. Now when I say successful, we sold over 100,000 of that album, and in those days it was an unheard-of figure in the gospel field."

It was the second album with the Angelic Choir however that really established him as the hottest act in gospel and earned him his first title as 'Crown Prince of Gospel'. Fred Mendelsohn remembered that session with undisguised pleasure too.

"Peace Be Still was also live, but Rev Roberts had razed his church and was building another one. So we recorded it in a Seventh Day Adventist Church as that was the only church not already in use on a Sunday. We got the crowds and it was a piece of magic. There too, you could feel the excitement running high and that's what makes an album. The inspiration was there."

It still stands as Cleveland's greatest work, selling over a million copies to make it the best selling gospel record of its time.

Gospel was now, finally, big business. Although James Cleveland was the very last person one would ever imagine connected to an enterprise like the Sweet Chariot, he nevertheless must be considered as one of the first major figures to become involved in the mass marketing of gospel. The essential difference between the two - quite apart from the financial motives and commercial results - is that Cleveland's market was almost totally confined to the African-American community. Since he was never concerned to dilute or package the product for white consumption, his contribution to the *internal*,

The late King of Gospel, Rev James Cleveland.

organisational strength of modern black gospel has been pre-eminent. Whatever he may have taken out of the church, he always re-invested massively in its people, its groups and its choirs. Nothing illustrates this more completely than the long nurtured ambition he fulfilled in 1968 when he convened the first of what was to become an annual Gospel Music Workshop of America. *"We have tried,"* he explained, *"to put our hands out to the many young people who have a desire to better themselves in gospel. We put together these classes where they could learn everything they wanted to know."* The influence of the Workshops - working in local chapters and in national convention - was phenomenal, spawning mass and community choirs right across the country. Cleveland's own project, the Southern California Community Choir, was fittingly the most renowned, due in great part to the patronage of his former protege Aretha Franklin, who recorded the most impassioned performances of her career with the choir on her double album *Amazing Grace*.

In business he was gruff and calculating, but on stage he became the flamboyant showman of gospel, a silk-suited catalyst growling his praises before massed ranks of be-robed altos, sopranos and tenors. Whether appearing alongside Jesse Jackson at PUSH concerts or as pastor of his $1.5 million Cornerstone Institutional Baptist Church in Los Angeles, he was always a towering presence amongst his people. He never crossed over to the wider, white market and he probably never wanted to, but his popularity with gospel music audiences - throughout the world - was unprecedented.

> *"James always did love the music,"* says one of his fellow Chicago singers, *"But I can remember when folks paid him no mind. He'd just go to everybody, begging them to let him sing on their programs. Remember, we had some singers back then. The folks weren't particular about that boy. Hmmm, he was so skinny then, he'd go begging us all for food off our plate. It wasn't nothing to see James anywhere, out there hustling. But it paid off, didn't it?"*

The long years of service and the indefatigable commitment did indeed pay off, earning for James Cleveland almost universal respect from all the regular church folks who embrace gospel music as the ordinary mode of their worship. It's they who bestowed on him the title 'King of Gospel' and it was evident that he took his majesterial responsibilities very seriously, descending without pomp to his subjects, ministering continually to all the choirs and artists who looked to him for guidance and support.

His was a benevolent patronage, as close to the grass roots of modern church-based gospel as it was to the pervasive traditions of the art. He was, for instance, just as eager to introduce me to the awesome vocal triumph of Vanessa Bell Armstrong's debut album as he was to talk over old times. His legacy lives on in the phenomenal current popularity of choir-based 'new traditional' gospel - John P. Kee, Hezekiah Walker and Kirk Franklin each owe a specific debt to the late great King James.

True men and women of the people are less rare in gospel than in other musics, but even within the select band of saints and survivors who dominate the modern scene, James Cleveland had perhaps the greatest ability to express the plain faith and exercise the common touch. He was just the big man of gospel and we all loved him for it. His homegoing service was in the Los Angeles Shrine Auditorium on 16th February 1991. The Caravans were all there; so too was Andrae Crouch, Tramaine Hawkins, Stevie Wonder and thousands of others who had lined up for hours to sing him home in a great chorus of *I'll Fly Away*.

As James used to say, *"If anyone should get round to writing my life story, tell them Jesus is the best thing that ever happened to me."*

Cleveland's regal counterpart of course is Shirley Caesar, the reigning First Lady of evangelistic gospel singing, whose personal calling card still bears the legend 'Down-To-Earth Singing For An Up-To-Date God'. It's an apt description of what Shirley does for a living but it demonstrates equally her delight in the snappy turn of phrase. Her conversation and her singing is peppered all the time with witty slogans, homilies and stock phrases - 'We're out to reach the lost, at any cost, for Pentecost.' Her audiences roar their appreciation. When she testifies to her Jesus, as she does most of the time, she unleashes a torrent of gospel couplets - *"He's my Rose of Sharon, my bright and morning star, my lily of the valley, my mountain mover ..."* For a lot of singers this would just be a routine they fall back on when things are drifting and the folks are getting restless. Shirley's particular genius lies in her ability to take a worn-out cliche and infuse it with the original power. It doesn't always quite work but, at her best, she's able to take just about any old truism and turn it into a pearl of great price.

It's something she couldn't pull off without that astonishing voice of hers. There's a rough kind of urgency in the way Shirley sings that leaves you in no doubt whatsoever that she's in deadly earnest. A lesser singer will sometimes coast along for effect, content to be applauded just for being on stage and staying in tune, whereas Shirley gives the impression that she could never sing two notes without hinting that the third might be her last. She's what you might call an eschatological singer - nobody sits comfortable, or immortal, while she's on.

She was born to be this kind of evangelist. Myrrh Records put the start of her career at the age of seventeen, but by that time she was already a hardened professional. At only ten years old she was singing with her sisters, Anne and Joyce, and a cousin Esther, as the Caesar Sisters, appearing at school and at her church The Love Calvary Holy Church. She first toured and recorded as Baby Shirley (she cut three sides for Federal in 1951 when she was only twelve) and later in the fifties as a duo with Leroy Johnson.

"Leroy was originally from Suffolk in Virginia and he has only one leg. When I met him he was a gospel radio announcer as well as a singer. I went to the station one Sunday with my Pastor for a radio service and he invited me to come back the following Sunday to sing on his programme. From there we started to sing as a duet and that's really how I first came to meet up with a lot of the top gospel singers."

The city of Durham in North Carolina is her home base. She was born there, one of twelve children, and she still lives there today, refusing to be drawn as so many gospel singers are to the big recording centres of Los Angeles or Nashville. Durham by contrast is in the heart of southern gospel territory and Shirley is about as down-home as you can get. The death of her father, Big Jim Caesar (a minister and the regular lead of the Just Come Four) dealt a disastrous blow to the family and Shirley was out singing to raise the rent before she entered her teens. The experience forged an unusually deep and extremely public bond between Shirley and her mother Hallie - celebrated often in her songs and in live appearances. After Jesus, her mother is her favourite topic of conversation, to the extent that she nominated the sickly-sweet *No Charge* to me as her favourite recording of all. It's a maudlin country music epic written by noted songwriter Harlan Howard and Shirley recorded her version using an all-white session band for the first time. The sentimental song contrasts the materialism of a modern child with the unselfish devotion of an idealised mother. Shirley is the child - but repentant:

> *"I felt that if I went out and sang as a child, why should I bring my Mum back all the money? Why should I have to take a nickel to school to buy a carton of milk and a biscuit? Why can't I buy hot lunches like everybody else? Back then my mother explained it; she said it was because she needed the money and because we were way down on the totem pole when it came to prosperity. See, I owed her everything but I didn't appreciate that fact. So I say that for all you may give to your mothers you still owe them something and when you add it all up the cost of real love is no charge."*

The recorded version of *No Charge* originally included Shirley's addition to the secular lyrics: '*...when I think about that, I think about the day that Jesus went out on Calvary and gave his life as a ransom for me. I think about the words: If any man be in Christ, he is a new creature. I like to think that the very minute that he shed his blood, my debt was paid in full.*' Scepter Records edited all this out and went for a non-gospel market, though they shrewdly tacked the full version on the **B** side, thus generating huge sales across the board. There were suggestions at that point that Shirley might take up a secular career, but she countered them in her inimitable way:

> *"Everybody knows that Shirley's hooked, an addict on gospel, and that I'm an evangelist. The USA doesn't have enough money to make me sing rock 'n' roll!"*

Like James Cleveland, Albertina Walker, Inez Andrews, Dorothy Norwood, Bessie Griffin et al, Shirley Caesar is a graduate of the famous Caravans.

> *"The Caravans came to our area to sing in July 1958,"* she told me. *"And I remember there was three of them - Albertina, Inez and Sarah McKissick. I was out of school and I didn't have any money to go back. I went to see them first in Raleigh, then when they left there that Sunday afternoon to go on to a little town called Kingston in North Caroline, I followed them. Sitting in the audience during their programme I wrote a request on a piece of paper and sent it up to them "Please call Shirley Caesar to sing a solo". And they did. I used the song The Lord Will Make A Way Somehow and Albertina Walker, who managed the Caravans, said "I want that little girl". After the programme she came up to me and said "Ask your mama if you can go with us". My Mum said yes, so I sold my biology book and I met them the following Thursday in Washington, DC."*

She spent eight glorious years with them, first as the opening act in their programme but quickly establishing her own reputation with fiery solos and blistering sermonettes. *"The Lord used the Caravans as a bridge to bring me to where I am today and I praise Him for that. They were happy days. I was the youngest and enjoyed the good and the bad."* The super-abundance of talent in the Caravans took them into the very front rank of gospel groups in the early sixties but it also generated an impossible pressure within the group itself. Eventually the constraints of the group proved too frustrating and Shirley broke out:

> *"I felt they weren't letting me use everything. I wanted to do something broader than just singing lead on my numbers. I wanted to go on and say something else, as God and the Spirit took me."*

Shirley Caesar, First Lady of Gospel.

The legendary Caravans: Albertina Walker, seated at piano with James Cleveland;
Shirley Caesar, back left.

Shirley Caesar, without the Caravans, took on the mission of travelling evangelist, holding revivals all over the country, preaching every bit as hard as she sang. The people - young and old - flocked to hear her and *"Then I came further in two years than in the previous eight"*. She began recording in her own name for Hob Records and produced a superb debut album for them called *I'll Go*, recorded with the Young People's Choir of the Institutional Church of God in Christ in Brooklyn. She scored a massive gospel hit with *Stranger On The Road* (duetting with sister Anne). Both records achieved gold status. Her 1969 sermonette, *Don't Drive Your Mama Away* took up the matriarchal theme Shirley is so attached to and turned herself into the heroine of every under-appreciated mother. (Another hymn of mother devotion appears on her Myrhh album *Rejoice* ... *"I just stood at the mike, closed my eyes, visualised my mother sitting there, and I talked to her ... I Love You Mama"*).

From Hob she went to Road Show Records, where they gave her the title 'First Lady of Gospel Music' but it was a difficult period. Though she wouldn't admit it at the time, she told me later of the hiatus they created in her career:

"When I got to the studio to record Shirley Caesar - First Lady, I found that they'd already laid the tracks and it was really rock music. Now here I am the same type of traditional gospel singer and never ever in my life had I sung to that kind of music. Now that's more the kind of stuff they're doing but then the church wouldn't accept it and so consequently it made my career be sort of at a standstill for a while. I was just singing gospel but the music was too far out for the churchgoers. I never had any control over it."

In a curious way it may have eventually worked to her advantage. As she joined the Christian label, Word Records, in 1979 she took with her the unearned reputation of an artist far ahead of her time. Coupled with her more proper identity as the uncompromising queen of down-home country gospel, she was able to extend her appeal to the widest audience. Almost like one of her own throwaway lines, Shirley Caesar today combines the best of the old with the best of the new.

In the hands of a lesser personality, that combination would end up as a very soft option - old time schmaltz mixed with tepid funk. Shirley's special qualities, transforming the most mundane and corny of songs, are to be found in her unique voice and her evangelistic commitment to a 'deliverance' ministry.

"I teach. I preach. I have a praying ministry. I have an altar in my home where I pray for hundreds and hundreds of people. I have a radio ministry every Sunday morning, 10-10.45 am on WSRC in Durham. God is doing his thing right from Durham, N.C. I don't have to move to a big city, big attorneys and this and that. The Lord chose this little spot where I'm home with my family. My ministry is more geared to the lowly ... to those really going through something, who are broke, busted, downtrodden and destitute ... really out of it. For some reason the Lord always gives me an answer for them. A girl came by my office the other day who was on her way to kill somebody and the Lord gave me a message for her. She was saved right then and there. Another girl last week in St Louis was getting ready to commit suicide. God gave me a word for her. Now she wants to live and live for Jesus. I have a person-to-person ministry. I'm not a star. You spell star backwards and it spells rats. I'll take time out and witness until they turn the lights out on me backstage. Our mightiest place should be at the feet of Jesus. The minute we get too high, the Lord brings us down."

Shirley Caesar came up from *'a long line of poor folk'* and retains an intimate relationship with the ordinary people in the gospel community, though she herself is now extremely wealthy. At her wedding in the early eighties, when she married Bishop Harold Ivory Williams of the Mount Calvary Holy Church, 2,500 fans turned up to the lavish and spectacular event and many of them stayed for a slice of the eight foot long wedding cake. The bride and groom sang their vows to each other, George Scott of the Original Blind Boys sang *One In A Million* and the Durham Youth Orchestra played *Pachelbel's Canon*. Not counting three officiating ministers, there were no less than 140 people in the wedding party, including three best men, 23 bridesmaids, 14 junior bridesmaids, 14 junior groomsmen, a complement of flower girls, train-bearers and candle-bearers, and two preschoolers acting the part of miniature bride and groom. Only the fog-machine, hired to provide a mist effect during the ceremony, refused to play its part in the Hollywood-style production. *"This wedding's costing me something like twenty-five thousand dollars,"* said Shirley, adding with a mischievous chuckle, *"But I've never been married before and I felt like this was a chance for me to feed the hungry and clothe the naked."* Hallie Caesar, the bride's mother and object of Shirley's undying devotion, sat fanning herself centre stage and fended off the man from the Washington Post. *"Don't you think she's entitled to it?"*, she demanded.

Shirley Caesar would be a bizarre anachronism were it not for the fact that she is supremely able to communicate great truths through her music. Hers is a populist gospel - the simple, unsophisticated faith of working men and women told in a raw, uncomplicated fashion. To those who don't know her, she might be taken for the kind of boot-legging evangelist who sells religion by the pound, but she's utterly genuine and the regal razzmatazz is just a side-show - her way of knowing how far up the rough side of the mountain she has come:

> *"Those that have come up the smooth side of the mountain will slip because they have nothing to hold on to. But because the Lord has taken me the slow and sure way I've learnt to use something special that you can't buy anywhere else. Any group that climbs to the top overnight, if they should fall there is no rock or twig, no branch, no nothing that they can hold onto."*

Shirley is unique in modern gospel music, seemingly able to draw upon all the strongest elements of the gospel tradition and weld them into a thoroughly contemporary and thrilling ministry. *"I can sing for any audience, whether they are young or old. I think it's a shame that many talented singers put themselves into a box. I'll sing for anybody who needs to hear the message I have to share."*

In terms of white understanding of African-American gospel, no-one has more actively crossed over in the past three decades than Andrae Crouch. Out of the self-proclaimed Jesus Movement of 60s disinherited evangelicals arose a demand for an overtly Christian counter-culture which manifested itself largely as music-with-a-message. At open-air festivals and in Christian coffee bars, through radio and records, a whole generation of young white Christians seized upon Andrae Crouch as a synonym for black gospel. It was something at which he worked consciously, toning down the emotional excesses of the gospel performance and absorbing the smooth pop sophistication of West Coast session singers.

Unlike James Cleveland, Andrae was happy enough to adapt to the white market as he made clear in an interview he did with the influential NBC programme Today:

"Sometimes you sing for white audiences and you know they're thinking 'Oh, these guys are going to be swinging from the chandeliers.' So I start out with something nice and easy (demonstrating on the piano), and after I get them warmed up, I can move to something like this ..."

Which would be fine if he were simply offering a starter to a substantial main course, providing a point of access to the uninitiated. The problem so often in the past with Andrae is that he wandered ever deeper into territory that delighted in bland and superficial music; so much so that after his nice and easy intro he would usually follow in with an equally nice and easy snack. Middle America in the seventies went overboard for it, just as they did exactly a century before with the Fisk Singers - and for pretty much the same sort of reasons.

In view of what he's said elsewhere on the subject, we ought to ask whether James Cleveland was merely being diplomatic when he told the (white) Gospel Music Association:

"Andrae Crouch has bridged the gap between black and white audiences ... The white artists are very interested in the more soulful type of gospel music ... In the contemporary sound of gospel music, many black musicians are now embracing the contemporary sound. There is a great upsurge of white choirs that sing like black choirs, and the blacks have always tried to excel and perfect performances relating to sound, arrangement and instrumentation. Orchestrations and the like bring us closer to what the white man has been doing all the time ... So they're coming our way and we're going their way. Somewhere in the middle of the road we're bound to run into one another!"

Andrae occupied that middle ground like nobody else, with the result that a lot of his early recordings sounded like a test-card soundtrack, though his roots go much deeper. His father, Rev Benjamin Crouch, ran a family cleaning business in East Los Angeles, conducting a spare-time ministry before setting up the Emmanuel Church of God in Christ with Andrae's great-uncle Samuel M. Crouch. With his twin sister Sandra - later to become a succesful gospel artist in her own right - he remembers 'playing church' at the age of eight, using a pie tin for a tambourine and a commode for a pulpit. At nine he got saved for real, through his father's preaching. *"I sat there in the audience listening. When he gave the invitation I went forward. I just felt so close to the Lord. I cried and cried. When everybody started singing, I was so happy jumping around that I split my new shoes!"*

Several months later his father had to decide whether or not to accept a pastorate at a church with no music director.

"One day in the service dad called me up front, laid hands on me and prayed 'Lord I don't know what you want me to do, but if you want me to be a pastor full-time, really give Andrae the gift of music.' He asked me, 'Andrae, if the Lord gives you the gift of music, will you use it?'"

Within two weeks the nine year old was sat at the piano bench and playing his first hymns. *"Dad kept his promise and took the pastorate. I played for all the services and later started a choir. At district meetings and youth rallies, I'd play the piano when I could."* It was a commitment made under duress though and privately he was looking for ways out. *"I never had any intention of going into the ministry because my folks were*

*Andrae Crouch and The Disciples at the height
of their popularity during the late 60s.*

Photo: Paul Slaughter.

pastors and I knew the hassles. I never wanted to live by 'faith' - that is, having to live on the support of people for everything."

Instead he toyed with teaching as his first career but dropped out to join 'Teen Challenge' - the fundamentalist organisation set up by Dave Wilkerson, author of *The Cross and The Switchblade*. At their Los Angeles rehabilitation centre for drug addicts, Andrae began to develop his songwriting skills:

> *"There the Lord really put a burden on my heart for people. I saw the effects of my music on people that didn't know the Lord and I began to write songs like A Broken Vessel and I Find No Fault In Him because there were a lot of troubles around at the time. I was spiritually moved and impressed because I could see the work of God ... miracles happened right before my eyes ... and how God used me!"*

He formed a choir with a group of ex-drug addicts and started performing with them around the Southern California churches. Although he'd already made some tentative stabs at gospel music in a group with sister Sandra and brother Benjamin Crouch Jr, this was the first time he'd really thought of a career as a gospel singer. *"We saw thousands come to the Lord, so that really launched it. I really had no intentions of full-time ministry but it just happened!"*

His first taste of recording was with the local **COGIC** Singers (who were also featuring Billy Preston) but it wasn't until he left 'Teen Challenge' and formed his first touring group that he began to issue records under his own name. *Take The Message Everywhere* was the first album issued in 1969 by Andrae Crouch and The Disciples and it sold well enough to establish them on the professional circuit. A successful second album eighteen months later (*Keep On Singing*) kept them in business and a prime spot on the Johnny Carson *Tonight* show brought them national fame overnight. By the time of their third album *Soulfully*, Andrae was already developing his persona as the acceptable face of progressive black gospel. In came the slick production techniques and publicists talking about 'a unique fusion of rhythm and blues, country, jazz and Latin rock.' Two huge radio hits resulted - *Everything Changed* and the neo-gospel *Satisfied* - firing Andrae with an ambition to cross over in all directions:

> *"I want to reach as many people as I can with my ministry and music. I want to take my music to people that have never heard the gospel. They have a right to hear it. A lot of times we don't promote our music like the secular field and I don't think that's fair."*

1974 saw him on stage at New York's Carnegie Hall in front of ten thousand devotees and though he was declaring *"we couldn't care less about recording a concert ... we had church"*, the subsequent live album proved to be his biggest promotional triumph so far. As gospel music itself began to be recognised in some quarters as a legitimate and viable form of modern show-business, so Andrae came to greater and greater prominence.

 A succession of best-selling albums followed, each more refined and lavish than the last, until the production techniques came to rival anything the **LA** session-machine could offer. On *This Is Another Day* he went the whole way, drafting in people like Joe Sample from the Crusaders and Leon Russell so that, lyrics apart, there began to be little to differentiate Andrae's style of gospel music from the predominantly bland

Andrae Crouch, perhaps the most influential figure in modern gospel music during the past thirty years.

Photo: Viv Broughton.

sounds of West Coast pop.

His songwriting completely redeems him and in this respect he compares directly with Thomas Dorsey. Like Dorsey, he was never a sweet-voiced singer, but as a writer he has composed a catalogue of truly great and timeless songs - nearly 600 at the last count. *Soon and Very Soon* and *Start All Over Again* are already beginning to enter into common congregational usage and *Jesus Is The Answer* became universally known through Paul Simon, who featured it heavily for years, earning for Andrae his first gold disc. *"I have one question when I write a new song: 'Does it reach you?' I feel the feedback from an audience if the song is working. I know what is real - that's what I get being raised in the church, before those congregations,"* he says.

In 1981 he disbanded the Disciples after losing mainstay Danniebelle Hall and founder member Billi Thedford and all future albums were credited solely to him. He still put together loose aggregations of singers for tours and for special occasions but the gruelling round of live shows was giving way rapidly to studio recording. With his long time drummer and co-producer Bill Maxwell he made a determined bid for commercial breakthrough to the national charts with *Don't Give Up* - a studio extravaganza involving just about every top LA session musician. Despite the backing of the giant Warner Brothers corporation, the album failed to impress pop fans and left Andrae with only the murmurs of church critics for having attempted it. To them he replied *"I believe the lyric of a song and the actual feel of the music are two different things. For example, by taking the infectious beat of Motown, the well-produced, innovative Philadelphia sound, the simplicity of Nashville or Muscle Shoals, and attaching it to the Lord's message, a lot of people are going to listen."*

If this was controversy, nothing could prepare the church for the thunderbolt which struck one cold night in December 1982. While his parents were away at a Church of God in Christ convention in Atlanta, one of the church deacons met up with Andrae at his Marina del Ray apartment. The intention was to go out for a meal but they never made it to the restaurant.

> *"When we got ready to leave, we were pulling out and I saw these police cars. In Marina del Ray they're always pulling people over. I'm a very cautious driver. I was getting ready to make a turn. I see this police officer on the side of me. Before I knew it their lights were on, I thought, 'What is this guy doing? I'm not speeding'. I was just totally blown away. So I pulled over. He said, 'You're Andrae Crouch aren't you?' The deacon pulls out a new album I'd just given him and says, 'Yeah, this is really him'. So it was just like a joke."*

The joke was over though when they searched the singer, claimed to have found an empty vial and arrested him for possession of cocaine. They held him for nearly ten hours until the deacon could arrange for the $2,500 bail. *"I kept going to sleep and waking up every 10 minutes,"* Andrae remembered. *"I thought it was possibly a dream, but I couldn't snap out of it. One of the other prisoners told me that God would pull me through. 'Just listen to your songs, man' he told me."*

Within a few days the district attorney dropped the charges for lack of sufficient evidence but the damage was already done. Sadly, it was not at all unusual for gospel singers to dabble in drugs - especially on the West Coast, where dope is as much an accepted stimulant as whisky - and there were many who shrugged their shoulders and presumed him guilty. Andrae's own explanation and detailed rebuttal of the claims were set out in a lengthy interview with the magazine *Contemporary Christian Music*. It allowed for only two possible conclusions. Either he was the innocent victim of a police frame-up (given what we now know about the **LAPD**, a distinct possibility) or he was repeatedly lying through his teeth. Surprisingly perhaps, in the light of their frequent criticisms of Andrae's worldly ways, the church gave him the benefit of the doubt:

> *"I got over 4,000 phone calls, thousands of letters and telegrams from around the world. If I had any fears that the church, the precious body of Christ, would come to me and say 'I told you so', those fears were blown away from the first day. 'Andrae is just like us,' it seemed like they were saying. 'He hurts like we hurt. He's a criminal ... we love him.' Suddenly, all the differences I'd ever had with the church just faded away. People who'd criticised my music the most were loving me!"*

It was a measure of the church's capacity for trust, even in extreme circumstances, but it doesn't (and shouldn't) preclude critical appraisal. The pursuit of opulent life-styles by a handful of top gospel singers sits as uneasily with the tenets of the Christian faith as any other vice. Andrae's empire had grown to become a massive global operation through his Crouch Ministries, run by the former head of the South African based 'Invisible Church'. His several palatial homes in California and Hawaii bore witness to the vast financial gains he had made from gospel music. Where people like Shirley Caesar and James Cleveland seemed to have retained a simplicity of faith as performers, despite all the trappings of fame, the same could not be said at that time for Andrae Crouch. There was a complacency in his music that was more a reflection of casual Californian values than the righteousness of African-American churches. He himself described his studio base as the 'laid-back laboratory of the Lord' and he became far more likely to be found alongside Pat Boone and Billy Graham than with fellow **COGIC** singers like the Clark Sisters.

In 1994, he finally came good, proving that you should never give up on a child of God. The Qwest album *Mercy*, is a complete triumph in every respect. Performance and production in a perfect symbiosis and the songs as good if not better than ever before. One, *The Lord Is My Light*, is destined to be one the greatest of all choir songs. After a long and difficult period of darkness and ill-health, he was back as a supreme gospel songwriter and minister, having also taken over the pastorate of his late father's church.

Where Andrae led, Jessy Dixon tended to follow. Like Andrae, he crossed over to the more lucrative white market - largely thanks to Paul Simon, who regularly featured the Jessy Dixon Singers in all his performances and recordings and even films - Jessy acted and sang in Simon's feature film *One Trick Pony*. For a while, he became every pop singer's favourite gospel flavour and he turned out regularly for Phoebe Snow, Leo Sayer, Diana Ross, Natalie Cole and Cher. The word was, that if you needed a bit of discreet gospel vocalising to liven up your act, Jessy was your man. It helped that he wasn't a Christian. Like some singers who earn a living singing gospel, Jessy Dixon sang without believing, which meant he could be relied upon to provide the facsimile without waving the original around in an embarrassing manner.

His origins were authentic enough. He was discovered in his native Texas by the Pilgrim Travellers, whose manager J. W. Alexander (also Sam Cooke's manager) set him up as accompanist to Brother Joe May - the 'Thunderbolt of the Mid-West'. His parents were less than delighted. *"My father was a Methodist and doing pretty good in business. My mother was Sanctified but she didn't approve of gospel - she wanted me to go to college and be a proper musician."* For a while he was dutiful, enrolling as a music major in his local San Antonio college, but James Cleveland passed through and offered him a job with the Gospel Chimes:

> *"My first professional engagement was at the Apollo Theatre and James Cleveland had me to work hard. He was headlining and he had some local acts - I think the Caravans were on that bill. I remember that James took me there from Chicago and I didn't know he was going to have me sing. I was so nervous I almost fainted! I sang There's a Brighter Day Ahead, a song which he had written."*

Cleveland took over where the San Antonio college was obliged to leave off and Jessy talks with great affection about his basic training:

> *"I was like an apprentice - I played the piano and Billy Preston played the organ. James would teach us and talk to us like a father. He'd tell us how to stand at the microphone and how to enunciate. He used to say, if I was in college I'd have to pay for this but he'd taken me on and was giving me money to sing. I thought I was rich, making twenty-five dollars a week! Then he took me to New Jersey, out to Savoy Records which was owned by this Jewish guy, Herman Lubinsky. He'd recorded the Davis Sisters and all these people and they liked my organ playing, so I played on the Roberta Martin Singers' albums. I was about eighteen then and much younger than them. One day Herman Lubinsky was in his office and heard me singing a song called There Is No Failure In God - this was from the studio two doors down - and he came out with his big cigar and asked who was singing. I was afraid to say it was me, I thought I'd done something wrong, but he said 'I'll record you on your own', and that's how I got started."*

It was the era of the big choirs and Savoy had already had their first smash hits with James Cleveland and the Voices of Tabernacle (*Love of God*) and the record breaking Angelic Choir (*Peace Be Still*). Where Cleveland led, his pupil Jessy Dixon was still bound to follow and he began a long association with the Chicago Community Choir.

> *"This was a choir which had something like a hundred voices - school teachers, nurses and people who didn't have anything to do at night, who wanted to sing in hospitals and jails and places like that. This wasn't for money, it was just as a hobby. Lubinsky asked me to use them on a record, which was a hit and we were asked to come to Carnegie Hall to sing gospel with James and Shirley Caesar."*

In many ways it's surprising that Jessy Dixon stayed with gospel. The pop attraction was ever present and he was keenly aware of the opportunity.

> *"I remember meeting Dionne Warwick in New York. We were both fans of gospel singers, though neither one of us was saved at that time. So we'd go around and listen to people like Marion Williams with the Ward Singers and Alex Bradford. These people made an impression on me and when the opportunity came for us to sing, Dionne chose secular music because she was doing background vocals. I was doing the same thing, I was playing on secular records but I didn't want to sing it."*

Even the way he dressed - cream-suited like an Ebony sales director - was something he got from Sam Cooke. *"Sam was with the Soul Stirrers when I was a little boy. He had such a manner about him, he was always very calm. He always had a suit on and he was always immaculate. I think I dress like him!"* Mahalia Jackson would have chuckled at that - she used to say that she always thought of Jessy Dixon as *"...the little boy with the runny nose."*

For a man who's got three gold albums to his credit, Jessy's recording career has been patchy in the extreme. Not that he's lacked the wherewithal, just that he seems never to have shaken off the 'young James Cleveland' tag. This, together with his lack of Christian conviction, has made for some half-hearted performances. It should by rights, have all changed in 1972 when he underwent a dramatic conversion. *"I was making a living singing,"* he says, *"It was all I knew how to do because it was all I had ever done. My singing was anointed, but I wasn't."* He'd put on a pretty good act over the years and was known to get happy in the spirit with little provocation, but the shouting and the fervour were a sham and some of the other singers were beginning to spot it. Not that they were all entirely blameless in this respect and it's to Jessy's credit that he at least came clean.

The immediate consequences of his conversion were a new record label and a testimonial album with the re-assuring title of *It's All Right Now*. Unfortunately, it wasn't. Jessy's soul may have been saved but his music continued to be losing to the suffocating confines of his adopted pop culture. Whatever may have happened to him spiritually, he sounded lazy and self-satisfied and this album stands out as such a low point that I was tempted to think it was actually an earlier recording. That suspicion grew with his second post-conversion album - *You Bring The Sun Out*, probably his finest 70s recording in every respect.

Throughout that decade, like Andrae Crouch, he would sing more often for white audiences than black and accept the limitations that were attached to the bigger pay-days. It was a subtle thing, but in return for a mass market he tacitly agreed to deliver a high quality acceptable product. This was relatively new for gospel music. The distinctly low-tech, and discomforting traditions had kept all of its best art outside of the entertainment mainstream, but things were changing. Now someone like Jessy Dixon could get the best arrangers, studios, musicians and producers that money could buy. He jetted around the world, stayed at the Hilton and enjoyed all the organisational back-up of a big record company. His part of the bargain was to write and sing songs that would sell and he was a conspicuous professional at the job. He would stroll into a TV studio looking like a man on holiday and execute a demanding song like *Through The Blood Of Jesus* in one take - with feeling but without drama.

There was a kind of triumvirate of superstars who worked this circuit, reaping its rewards and putting up with its occasional indignities: Andrae, Jessy and the Hawkins family. To them though, and particularly to Edwin Hawkins, must go the credit for opening up a world constituency for contemporary gospel music in the last quarter century.

It all began to happen back in 1969 in Oakland, California, when the teenage Edwin got involved with the community choir based at his Ephesian Church of God in Christ. Calling themselves the Northern California State Youth Choir, they began preparations to represent northern California at the Youth Congress in Washington DC. To raise funds for the church they cut an album and included the old Baptist

*Edwin Hawkins with
(inset) The Edwin Hawkins Singers in 1976.*

hymn *Oh Happy Day*. Edwin was a student of interior design and totally unprepared for what happened next. *"I'd almost completed the curriculum when my whole life turned in a new direction."* Out of nowhere the record began to assume the proportions of a hit:

> *"We cut it privately by a local recording enterprise who turned out 500 records the first order. The next order for 1,000 also sold quickly. Then things began to happen. A young man who worked in the warehouse used by the non-commercial recorder (Century Records) took the record to the underground rock station KSAN in San Francisco. Shortly afterward, the record hit in 'Frisco - then New York. This was God's blessing on our ministry."*

By Easter of that year, the Hawkins family were being inundated with offers from every major record company in America. The choir went professional, the record got repackaged and the re-named Edwin Hawkins Singers found themselves with a No.1 worldwide smash hit.

Completely bewildered by it all, the Oakland church choir - 56 singers plus 22 chaperones - were flown to New York for their first national concert, at the gigantic Madison Square Gardens. Yankee Stadium was next, for the Isley Brothers' anniversary celebration, but the pressure was too great for some and by the end of the year the choir was down to 22 rapidly hardening professionals:

> *"Then we began doing lots of rock concerts and festivals. Coming from our Christian background, we weren't sure rock festivals were right to be involved with. We'd been taught not to associate with that part of the world. To see if it was God's will to perform at festivals, we started gathering daily for prayer."*

It's doubtful if the Lord's mandate extended quite as far as a tour of the Playboy circuit or the Las Vegas casinos but that was where they went. The folks back home in the church were up in arms but Tramaine Hawkins still feels it did more good than harm and rejects the obvious criticisms.

> *"Although scripture says that the Gospel should be taken to the highways and hedges, they didn't really consider clubs as highways and hedges,"* she says. *"A lot of times I felt the people in clubs were there to party and tuned us out, but a lot of people come to clubs or bars to find some kind of companionship or empty their problems out, and we were up there ministering and singing the same songs we would in church. Nothing new, nothing different. It was the same gospel and I know a lot of people were touched."*

Tramaine met and married Edwin's brother Walter in the group and the three of them became valuable recording property. The album *Tramaine* for instance sold 75,000 in 60 days. Tramaine Hawkins had started out singing in her grandfather's church at four and joined the Heavenly Tones three years later. With them she recorded a Savoy album (*I Love The Lord*) and travelled up and down the West Coast until she was fifteen. Sly Stone made them a handsome offer and they crossed over to become his backing group Little Sister but Tramaine bowed out saying *"I knew this wasn't for me"*. She joined Walter Hawkins' first group, Praisers of God, when she was sixteen and also organised the Progressive Three with Walter's sister Lynette and Gail Smith. She's done two stints with the Edwin Hawkins Singers and one with Andrae Crouch and the Disciples. She got engaged to Walter during an appearance by the choir at Caesar's Palace in Las Vegas and married him in March 1971.

Both Tramaine and Walter spent time in Los Angeles attempting secular recording careers for a while but it didn't work out. *"I just really couldn't get into it. There was no feeling there like I can get in gospel ..."* is Tramaine's brief comment but Walter is more forthcoming about it:

> *"I grew up in church and got to the point where I started rebelling against some of the set-up,"* he says. *"I started my own group from the Edwin Hawkins Singers and started doing night clubs because I wanted to do secular music for a while, but I couldn't break the ties because everything I was writing was really Christian orientated as far as lyrics were concerned. And even the people I was meeting in night clubs, we'd sit down and start to converse and we'd end up talking about God."*

The same year he married Tramaine, Walter Hawkins took a Master of Divinity degree and a year later became an ordained minister in the Church of God in Christ. Mrs Mamie Hawkins was beside herself with joy. Like any good **COGIC** mother, she'd kept her children off the Oakland streets by immersing them in church and she'd always wanted to see one of them ordained. Walter reciprocated with his tribute to her memory - at the back of his church is a shiny wooden chest full of books that carries the plaque 'Mamie Hawkins Memorial Library'.

By 1976, Rev Walter Hawkins was emerging as the new star of the family and his Love Alive album released that year stayed at the top of the Billboard gospel chart for over forty consecutive weeks, selling more than 300,000 copies for Word Records. He did almost as well with the two follow-ups, *Jesus Christ Is The Way* and *Love Alive II* and he invested the proceeds into his own Love Centre Church in East Oakland. His friends were sceptical of his new-style store front ministry:

> *"They thought it was just a passing phase. All they could see was me singing all the time. But God has blessed our work. To be a minister is much more rewarding and more fruitful than music alone. We see people of all denominations responding to the message of our church. I look to God to mesh the talents of my music with my calling to preach."*

On the road they were billed as 'Walter and Edwin Hawkins and the Family', and they all gave high priority to establishing the Love Centre church and its music ministry. It's a non-denominational, charismatic out-reach and it roused up further criticism from traditionalists. *"We made our appeal to people who were probably normally rejected by other churches because they didn't look like they belonged or because others thought it would ruin their church's reputation ... I don't think we have a reputation to protect ... we're not deal-ing with ceremony, we're dealing with people's real feelings."* (In 1981, the whole family ran into massive con-troversy for performing at a Gay Rights rally in San Francisco. It was Walter's decision to allow the choir and family to perform, but Edwin backed him all the way:

> *"I felt it was necessary. Anywhere there's a door open to take the Message in gospel song, we should do it. We're ministers of the Gospel, ... I still don't know why the Christian world makes a distinction between the music ministry and the preaching or speaking ministry. I think a preacher would or should go any-where he had an opportunity to preach and reach souls. Why can't musicians do the same thing?"*)

Walter sums up his attitude with a prayer: 'Let us be spiritual dynamite, Lord, not just mediocre.'

Tramaine Hawkins, in full flight.

Later, Edwin Hawkins took to working the opposite end of the economic spectrum with the very first attempt to mix gospel with classical orchestras. In September 1979, the family found themselves on stage with the National Symphony Orchestra at the John F. Kennedy Centre for the Performing Arts and they continued the experiment with a *Gospel at the Symphony* album with the Oakland Symphony Orchestra. Edwin described it as *"...God's door to reach a totally different segment of society with the Good News. They're not a church-orientated crowd who ordinarily respond to gospel music. They're the symphony crowd, the sophisticates who would not darken the door of a church."*

The move up-market seemed to have gone to the head of their manager/sociologist (his description, not mine!) Dwight McKee, who came over all pompous at the Kennedy Centre: *"Because Washington is the focal point of the world artistically and politically, it was only feasible to present and institutionalise this exciting concept before the White House, the National Black Caucus, the National Council of Arts and other cultural and religious leaders. We can now transcend cultures by presenting this new art form in concert everywhere we go."*

Fortunately, the music transcended the exciting concepts of Dwight McKee but it was a close run thing. Real musical fusions just don't happen at this level of high culture; if they happen at all it's always as an accident of cross-fertilisation, just as the first spirituals were themselves created. If a Committee for the Arts had been set up in the eighteenth century charged with the task of combining Isaac Watts' hymns with traditional African vocal music, you can be pretty sure they would not have produced anything remotely like a spiritual. (The classical/gospel fusion of the Richard Smallwood Singers in the 80s was much more successful, both artistically and commercially.)

The symphonic excursion of the Hawkins family was less of a deviance if you review the whole scope of their entertaining ministry. They've always presented their Christian religion as great popular show-people would and one avenue of dramatic spectacle became just as useful as another. Edwin Hawkins would use hit records to evangelise and he'd use the national Symphony Orchestra to the same end:

> *"I think many Christians fear some important words such as 'concert', 'performance', or 'show'. But we have to realise that this is a business too, and people are paying money to come and see a performance ... to see a show. The result has to come from the artists on stage, from their motives and objectives, and ours is to minister. At the same time, we want people to be entertained ... entertained by the Spirit."*

Of all the Hawkins family though, none eventually rose higher in the gospel firmament than the elegant soprano Tramaine. Her predilection for glitz and glamour drew some extreme criticism in the 70s and 80s - when earrings, fancy nails and make-up were frowned on by many of the churches. Nowadays, some gospel gatherings are a bit like an Essence fashion show but back then Tramaine Hawkins was *"...always pushing the envelope"* as Teresa Hairston of *Gospel Today* magazine puts it. Having built up an extensive audience, first with the *Love Alive* classic songs *Going Up Yonder* and *Changed* and then with her first two solo albums, she almost blew it completely in 1986 when she cut the song *Fall Down* for A&M Records as part of the album *The Search Is Over*.

Fall Down was put together for her by a dance music production team and was about as radical a piece of gospel music as had ever been recorded up till then. Tramaine put the vocal over in one take and it still holds up today as a superlative slice of commercial, contemporary hard gospel (becoming the first gospel record to hit No.1 on the Billboard dance charts) but she was devastated by the response from her traditional fans.

> "Church people thought I had left the church!" she exclaims. "I felt very bruised from the Christian market and audience. I didn't understand why there was so much criticism, and seemingly a real dislike for what I did. I didn't understand it because I really did it for ministry and my commitment to the Lord hadn't changed and I am still hearing testimonies from young people who came to the Lord through hearing 'wake up singing hallelujah, in the morning time'."

As a contemporary gospel pioneer, Tramaine has always been willing to take risks but, as she ruefully points out: "I listen to what the Winans and BeBe and CeCe are doing now and I say hey, at least I was saying 'Jesus' in the music. Now they just say 'He'. But I'm thankful to God, He's given me a tough upper lip. I'm able to stand, and through the pain, I come out stronger."

At 44, her marriage to Rev Walter Hawkins is now over, following an agonising, much-gossiped-over divorce. If you met her now, you would find an unlikely revolutionary, a woman of great resolve and purpose, stylish and beautiful, quietly generating one controversy after another. Tramaine's 1995 album *To A Higher Place* saw yet another twist to the Tramaine tale. Teaming up with orchestral legend Marty Paich and employing the lavish production skills of David Foster, she created an album that at first hearing was more Streisand than Sanctified and, once again, her fans were puzzling over the career moves she makes. What they no longer questioned though, was her personal integrity. From the age of eight, when she went on the road with her revivalist aunt, Tramaine has taken whatever the world (and sometimes the church) has thrown at her and turned it into a series of object lessons - scenes from the life of a modern pilgrim.

Andrae Crouch and the Hawkins family broke the mould of gospel music during the 70s and 80s. They governed what will come to be seen as a middle period for gospel, when the unique qualities of the music appeared to be in terminal decline. Many in gospel became disenchanted with the loss of clear direction and purpose and concluded that the glory days were over. They were wrong. In truth, the whole genre was in a state of flux. Huge social and musical changes were taking place throughout the world and gospel could never remain unaffected by them. A new generation was growing up in the urban churches of America who would overturn the heritage and invent a body of work as radical and challenging as any that had gone before.

In 1972 came a John the Baptist figure. The movie *Wattstax* featured a young unknown from Monroe, Michigan, with his two brothers, alongside the established names of soul and gospel like the Staple Singers. Rance Allen's astounding voice scared everyone else on the bill half to death and he became a seminal influence on an upcoming generation of gospel artists. If anyone led the avant garde of urban contemporary gospel, it was the singer who is known today as Elder Rance Allen of the New Bethel Church of God in Christ in Toledo, Ohio. No-one had driven gospel music to the outer limits the way that he did.

Rance Allen was way ahead of his time. Nowadays they seek out his long deleted albums and give him maximum respect but back then, he was the voice of one crying in the wilderness. ❖

Elder Rance Allen.

*The Maestro, the late Minister Thomas Whitfield,
composer, artist, producer.*

SWEEPING THROUGH THE GATES

The Last Days of Gospel Music

"Now that gospel music is selling like everything else, and more money is involved and finally we are able to use better equipment - state of the art technology - to get our messages out there, and use the rhythm and harmonies developed by us, we are accused of going 'mainstream'.
Hey, it's God's music, period!"
CeCe Winans

Thomas Dorsey finally passed over into glory on 23rd January 1993, outliving Rev James Cleveland by just two years. The gospel music industry these two men left behind has grown into a huge corporate business, today estimated to account for 10% of all US record sales - evangelism and entertainment co-existing in a sometimes uneasy symbiosis. In this sense, it is now what it has always been, certainly throughout the eras spanned by Dorsey and Cleveland. The major figures who currently dominate the contemporary gospel scene have all had to learn how to take care of business, how to project an image, how to market a product, how to build a professional organisation. The fact that the product is a type of Christian music makes little difference. The God that gospel singers today sing about is the same God that brought deliverance to the captive slave, but today it seems, He needs a higher brand profile.

Whether they're great survivors from a glorious past like Shirley Caesar, Andrae Crouch and Albertina Walker or youngbloods like Kirk Franklin, John P. Kee and Yolanda Adams or returned prodigals like Al Green and Helen Baylor, they're all faced with the same dilemma: is it possible in the 90s to sing gospel music without turning faith into a commodity?

There are some who choose not to play the game, performing only at church concerts and conventions with little attempt to sell product to the outside world or advance a career. And they're by no means the minor talents. Perhaps the single most spectacular voice of the 90s is Shun Pace Rhodes from Atlanta's Church of God In Christ and she is typical of many (her eight sisters for instance) who are church singers first and foremost. She records for Savoy, she won the 1994 Stellar Award for Best New Artist but she is also the most humble and un-starstruck of performers. She recalls how, in her early days at a COGIC Convention, she was unceremoniously hauled off the stage by Mattie Moss Clark, allegedly for not singing well enough. "Although it was harsh, it was done with love. She used to call me and my sisters, her daughters."

Vanessa Bell Armstrong was another Mattie Moss Clark protege, who went to middle age, brought up five children and served her church in Detroit without ever doing much more than guest vocals on a few records. She finally got to do an album of her own and took the opportunity to make what was certainly the most important gospel record of 1984 - Peace Be Still, produced by the late Thomas Whitfield. The major secular record deal with Jive that followed, opened her up immediately to the dilemmas of the modern gospel business and there were many who accused her of selling out.

The relationship between religion, art and business is more exacting in gospel music now than it has ever been. Some gospel singers manage to get one or other of the elements right; more singers than might be imagined get two of them right; but there are precious few who can claim integrity and excellence in all three. Shirley Caesar gets pretty close, despite being the first gospel artist to sell on the shopping channel QVC. Her evangelistic commitment is beyond question and her music is as eloquent as it is stirring. She's also a very shrewd businesswoman, taking a business studies degree at Shaw and passing out with honours:

> "As my businesses expanded, I knew that I was going to need some more business knowledge for my own publicity company, my booking agency, my outreach ministry and for our food programmes. When I was in high school they told me not to go to college, don't use up your mother's money they said. All those years when I was in the Caravans, I was riding in the car and I'd look out and see all those kids coming to and from school and my heart said, go back there. So now I have."

The artists themselves may see this differently, since they're the ones who've suffered the short-changing and the down-grading over the years, but it's likely that the faith and the music will always need to take precedence over the business if the heart of gospel is to remain healthy. It's not just coincidence that the golden age of gospel music was accompanied by the greatest level of marketing ignorance. While there's no sense in wishing for a return to those desperate days, there are more than a few singers who turned the whole thing on its head during the 80s, who refused to move a muscle or sing a note without a massive fee payable a third in advance. These new financial priorities for some gospel artists sprang from the rise of the so-called 'health and wealth' doctrine, espoused by sections of the right-wing evangelical churches. Put crudely, the doctrine teaches that God will reward 'good' Christians with the best of health and mater-

Photo: Sharron Wallace.

Vanessa Bell Armstrong.

ial riches. The converse of the doctrine is therefore implied, though not explicitly stated: that in this world, the poor and sick are that way because they are living lives that are disobedient to God. The doctrine is one of this century's greatest heresies, but it has an obvious appeal to wealthier Christians - TV evangelists and successful Christian recording artists among them. Competence and good order in business dealings is one thing; hustling for major bucks under the guise of Christianity is quite another. Fortunately, this kind of excess is the exception rather than the rule and most artists now strike a fairly healthy balance between their faith, their music and their business.

Like the Clark Sisters for instance. Back in June of 1983, these five sisters from the Detroit Church of God in Christ slipped quietly into London with their mother Mattie, spent several days shaking up the diaspora churches and flew out again. If you weren't already in on the British gospel circuit you wouldn't have known they'd been there at all. They were, at the time, America's premier female gospel act, and two months later, the rest of the world woke up to them through the cross-over single *You Brought The Sunshine*. The song was already a big dance floor hit in America through the plugging of ace New York jock Frankie Crocker and in Europe it also notched up healthy sales and massive airplay. Soon the Clark Sisters were being hailed in the hip music press as 'the rootsiest, throatiest black music act of the year' and Twinkie Clark as 'nothing short of a musical genius of soul'.

Twinkie is Elbernita Clark, the powerhouse songwriter and musician behind the group until she quit in 1989. I interviewed her just after the single broke through to the commercial market and their experiences were to become familiar to many others:

> "Our singing is our ministry and having a hit just means we can minister to a wider audience. Now we're drawing secular crowds as well as church people and we play auditoriums as well as churches now. Quite a few of the people in our church were shaken up by the crossover because we were being played in the bars and the clubs and on the rock stations. There's been a lot of criticism but at the same time we know that young people have gotten saved by hearing the record in bars and clubs. I think the church is just going to have to be more open minded, because these kids are the ones that need our ministry. These are the last days and the word has to get out before the return of Jesus Christ."

The Clark Sisters at that time - Karen, Jackie, Dorinda, Neicy and Twinkie - ranged in age from 24 to 36 and all learnt to sing at the knee of gospel legend Mother Mattie Moss Clark, the formidable but charming International Music Director of the Church of God in Christ. Mattie was born in Selma, Alabama in 1925, settled in Detroit, worked on the Chrysler assembly line, almost went into blues but committed absolutely to gospel music in her twenties.

> "It all started with my mum," said Twinkie. "She's recorded about 28 albums since 1958 and is the recipient of three gold records. She drilled us, she trained us and raised us in the church. My father was the pastor and we started first singing in the choir and then later I began accompanying my mother - we're all a close family group." Niecy puts it more bluntly, "We're like the Jews, we like to keep it in the family."

The Clarks believe in starting young. Mattie Moss was playing for COGIC at six years old and launched her daughters when they were even younger:

Photos: Rupert Francis/
Author's collection.

The late Dr Mattie Moss Clark, International Music Director of the Church of God in Christ, and mother of the Clark Sisters. Inset: Karen, Mattie Moss and Twinkie.

"If I had a song come to me in the middle of the night, I'd even get them all out of bed to try it out! The youngest was only two and a half ... I used to stand them on a table to sing."

Mattie Moss (sister of Bill Moss of The Celestials) claimed to have been the very first to record a gospel choir - the Michigan State Community Choir - though there might be a few counter claims to that distinction. Her first self-penned song was *Going To Heaven To Meet The King* which appeared on her debut Savoy album. The punishing schedules and public commitments back then took their toll of her personal life and she parted from her minister husband: *"We've been divorced for fourteen years now. You see I practically raised these girls single-handed."* Niecy chipped in, *"It comes from being on the road. Some men cannot adapt to the life we have, going where the Lord tells us to go ... even though we are married to them, our lives are not our lives, our lives belong to Jesus Christ and he's the master."*

Niecy was just as keen to declare the family's independence of the commercialised aspects of contemporary gospel:

"What we do is not like what everybody else does. They have their little songs that they sing, but we allow the Holy Ghost to totally take control. We project what God gives us, as the anointing falls on us, as the spirit falls on us, we act in that manner. Where a lot of people are very rehearsed, we are not rehearsed. I mean they come out and have a set thing to do and they will go through that set procedure. We don't work like that."

After Mattie Moss, Twinkie Clark was the compositional genius behind the group. If she were in secular music she might quite easily come to be recognised as one of the greatest artists in any genre. She studied music at Harvard as well as in church, she is possibly the funkiest keyboard player around, she has a voice like distilled fire and she writes the kind of songs that would turn any sinner's head. *You Brought The Sunshine* got them to a mass audience but the real masterpieces are songs like *Endow Me* (*'I really felt the glory of the Lord come in the room as I wrote that song'*) or *My Soul Loves Jesus* from her stunning solo album *Power* - far and away the most adventurous gospel recording of the 80s.

It's not all divine inspiration though. Twinkie has a thing about TV commercials and isn't above weaving jingle fragments into a song. *'You know that song we did called Jesus Had A Lot To Give? Well, there's a bit in there that goes (sings) 'the devil is trying to conquer you, he's been at you very long'. Now that's from the Pepsi Cola advert,"* says Niecy, laughing. *"And 'Oh triumph ...' is the Alka Seltzer tune. She's got the Macdonald's commercial in another song too if you listen hard!"* They repaid the compliment by doing one of their own for Sunny Delight Orange Juice. If they weren't so evidently genuine in their religious commitment, this might come over as a cheap shot for easy money. In their case, it's just a humorous throwaway, a tongue-in-cheek interlude.

There's certainly nothing coy or half-baked about Mattie Moss's daughters. They give of themselves in a way very few modern gospel groups care to, whether it's within the church - they run their own music Conservatory in Detroit and teaching workshops across the country - on record or live in front of an audience. At the heart of their operation throughout the 80s stood the matriarchal figure of Mattie Moss Clark, with a reputation for severity so great that many choir singers were terrified to work under her.

"Some people didn't understand Mama," Niecy countered quickly. *"They said she's hard core, they said she could make a little dog creep ... but she laboured. She was a perfectionist - just doing it wouldn't do. She spent most of her time reading scriptures. It's vital that we can pick up the same identical thing, because we are a blood family and we fill each other. We could rehearse with a band and do it her way and then the spirit came upon her, it hit her and her hands became anointed. She had a saying, that Jesus is the baddest man in town and we just follow his footsteps."*

Mattie Moss Clark's contribution to gospel music was truly immense and for me she ranks alongside James Cleveland as the other parental architect of the modern choir sound. In Atlanta, shortly before her death in 1994, the COGIC National Music Choir sang in her honour. Seven minutes into their spectacular performance of her epic (and last) composition *Be Still And Know That I Am God*, Mattie Moss Clark, frail from a stroke and wheelchair-bound after losing both legs, took the microphone and sang the text in a thin, fractured voice that moved every younger heart in the hall to tears. A few months later, she was gone and Donald Vails was paying tribute to the great Mother of COGIC music: *"She was one of the first to come with the hard-breaking, 'knock-em-dead' style of gospel music. People came from far and wide to Detroit just to sing with Dr Mattie Moss Clark. She gave many of us our start in gospel music."*

The significance of the Clark Sisters lies in the undiluted spirituality of their performances. While much of the rest of gospel music in the 80s slipped into lifeless production formulas, their divine vocal chorus regenerated the inspired, righteous, anointed tradition. Twinkie Clark in particular discovered how to be years ahead of her time by going right back to the biblical roots of the music. Like her mother, she could take a simple benediction like 'Now unto Him who is able to keep you from falling ...' and transform it into a majestic opus of breathtaking musical dimensions. At the same time she wasn't above throwing a line like 'God's economics beats Reaganomics' into another song. With gospel music at that time tending to imitate the drab predictability of 80s soul and funk, Twinkie (now Twinkie Clark-Terrell) had made the quantum leap that gospel desperately needed. This was a visionary act on her part because it placed gospel once again out in front of other music as being of infinitely greater significance - artistically as well as spiritually.

The focal point of gospel by this stage was moving emphatically to Detroit and, across town from the Clark's, another family was about ready to turn the music upside down.

Andrae Crouch had many disciples throughout the 70s and 80s. It's difficult to over-emphasise the influence of Andrae, and the Hawkins family, on that particular generation of young gospel artists. And few were more influenced than those church teenagers growing up in the auto-metropolis of Detroit - already bursting with the music of Mattie Moss and the Clark girls, home to Rev C.L and Aretha Franklin, and the proving ground for the secularised gospel sound that Berry Gordy created for his clutch of Motown superstars:

"When I was a child, Stevie Wonder lived on Greenlawn, which was a block behind us. We lived on Wooding and Smokey Robinson lived on Santa Barbera in front of us, the Four Tops lived on San Juan, and I used to pass Gladys Knight's home on the way to Junior High School. In this town there was just a sense of hope, that everybody had the opportunity to be a star."

Top: Karen, Dorinda and Jacky - the Clark Sisters.
Below: Twinkie Clark-Terrell.

Photos: Ebony/Viv Broughton..

The speaker is Marvin Winans - pastor, singer, songwriter and high profile leader of The Winans, four brothers who took gospel music by the scruff of the neck in the late 70s. The Winans' surname was to become synonymous with contemporary gospel, cutting a dynastic swathe through the music and the industry for the next twenty years.

David and Dolores Winans, known to everyone as Mom and Pop, met singing in a community choir ("*I used to try and sing like the Davis Sisters. They were my favourite,*" says Delores) and were married in 1953. He was 19, she was 21. The day after the wedding, Pop was laid off his job. "*We were young,*" says Pop. "*We had faith and the Lord supplied the strength. We had to do without a lot, but there were more joys than hard times. The good days outweighted the bad.*" There in Detroit, they raised a family of ten children, each of whom became successful gospel recording artists. It got started with Marvin and Marvin got started with a revelation - the Edwin Hawkins' version of *Oh Happy Day* hit him like a ton of Semtex in 1969:

> "*I remember when that record came out like it was yesterday. Happy Day. Now remember, this is an old hymn of the church. But because it got played on secular stations ... I can remember sitting in church and this old mother saying '...Mmm, it's a shame. They're saying Good God on that record.' And I'm, what, eleven, twelve? I'm saying, 'what's wrong with saying Good God? He's a good God ain't he?' They went berserk, I mean, they went ballistic!*"

Marvin's younger sister Priscilla (better known now as CeCe Winans and with brother BeBe, a five-time Grammy Award winner) recalls the formative sounds of the Winans' family home: "*Growing up, we had a piano in the house and mom and dad taught us songs for church. Don't forget, this was a God-fearing home - music was strictly for the church, for his worship and praise. We weren't allowed to listen to secular music....*" CeCe breaks off in mid-sentence and chuckles:

> "*OK, now let's get real. You couldn't possibly live in Detroit at that time and not hear the Motown sound. It was in the air you breathed. If the truth be told, it wasn't that alien to us. The church had the beat that secular music appropriated and also the synthesisers and other instruments. That's why it's so funny when people talk about the Saints singing secular music.*"

The Winans siblings, caught between the traditional rock of gospel and the Motown hard place, found a blessed middle ground in the music of Edwin Hawkins and unsurprisingly, Andrae Crouch. "*The first time we met Andrae was like...I wanna say '72, '73, and I was just blown away,*" says Marvin. "*That was the first time in my life that I'd ever seen whites and blacks worshipping in a concert setting. He had whites and blacks in his band and he was just, impressive, he was just anointed. I mean he spoke to everybody. When he played it was just inspiring and so I said 'man, I wanna do that'.*"

Marvin, Carvin, Ronald and Michael Winans formed themselves into a vocal quartet with no discernible reference back to the earlier quartet traditions in gospel. In fact, they seemed at the time to be almost consciously distancing themselves from the four-part lineage of previous male gospel groups:

> "*I think the problem with gospel music, and I think it permeates into Christian thinking generally, is that we think we must must guard something and regard the past as sacred. You know, I'm just not a religious*

Mom, Pop and the whole Winans family.

fellow. I'm not interested in icons and relics. I don't think the church was ever meant to be a monument, I think it was called to be a movement."

The Winans were controversial in gospel. Still are. Having stirred up the Michigan COGIC circuit, they finally caught the ear of their mentor Andrae Crouch, who hooked them up to his production company and a deal with Light Records. The string of best-selling albums that followed were unlike anything that had gone before in gospel but the group immediately ran into familiar-sounding controversy, when they were accused of bringing secular styles into the church. Marvin was militant in their defence:

"I never really consider us a real risque group or understand how so many would write about us as being controversial. The idea of traditional gospel versus contemporary gospel is a ridiculous notion in itself. We're all on the same team. You have those who play differently, but we all want to express the joys and message of our Lord Jesus Christ. I don't expect 'It's Time' to be sung as the preacher's marching in. It was written for young folks who are unchurched and I wanted to make it palatable."

BeBe and CeCe Winans, seventh and eighth amongst the siblings, were next out of the Detroit starting gate. Where their four brothers had marked out new territory, BeBe and CeCe set up permanent camp, launching their debut Sparrow/Capitol album in 1987. Their soft-focus style and Keith Thomas' super-slick production was an immediate hit with both black and white Christian audiences, garnering them two radio chart No.1's in *I.O.U. Me* and *For Always*. The follow-up album *Heaven* did even better, becoming only the second gospel recording to be certified platinum since Aretha's *Amazing Grace* in 1972 and picking up two Grammy's, four Dove Awards, four Stellar Awards and an NAACP Image Award. Subsequent albums *Different Lifestyles* (featuring close friend Whitney Houston) and *Relationships*, continued with this winning formula, consolidating their position as gospel's major cross-over artists. Now they were a bona fide music business phenomenon.

If their brothers had attracted criticism and controversy, it was nothing compared to the shots aimed in the duo's direction. *"BeBe and CeCe Winans have nearly perfected a slippery trick,"* wrote Jamie Lee Rake of *Contemporary Christian Music Magazine* in October 1994. *"They sing about God, sell millions of records doing so, don't often mention Him by name, yet have enough support from both gospel and R&B camps to top both album charts. A good part of that trick is in the presentation. Their message is often couched in the double entendres of God-as-lover songwriting."* CeCe returns fire with a patience born, one feels, out of much practice: *"We feel bad when people don't understand what we're doing, but you kind of get used to it. We can't apologise for what God has called us to do, but we can understand that everyone won't always like it ..."* while BeBe adds:

"There was a time people believed at funerals you always had to wear black. I remember my grandmother's funeral - before she left, her request was for all of us to wear white. And we did because it was a celebration. Our passing here is going from death to life. When it's planted in people's minds to think a certain way, it's hard for them to accept change, therefore they relate change to something other than good."

Bebe and CeCe are these days based in Nashville, where traditional and contemporary gospel don't always see eye to eye. Dr Morgan Babb, who used to lead the great Radio Four quartet in the 50s, now runs

Photos: David Corio/Author's collection.

The four Winans brothers take London by storm in 1984;
inset: BeBe and CeCe Winans.

Nashville's **WMDB** radio from a converted trailer in the less fashionable part of town - pumping out traditional gospel to a highly partisan audience:

"To me, the kind of gospel music they're producing today is too weak to pull a people through a struggle, it's not strong enough. It's like taking medication for hyper-tension and it's not strong enough to keep your blood pressure down. You never used to hear of so many black people committing suicide as you do today. They'd go to church, sing, pray, shout, cry, run, holler, and go right back and suffer some more of what they just suffered. But that's not true now."

If, in the past, traditional gospel artists were occasionally seduced into the secular mainstream, contemporary gospel music would seem to be far more ripe for the taking. The 80s saw a huge rise in the phenomenon known as 'inspirational music', whereby gospel singers could just about have it both ways. The line between sacred and secular was increasingly blurred, both musically and lyrically. Tramaine Hawkins was there with the scorching dance track *Fall Down* and lost an army of church support in the process; the Clark Sisters, incorruptible in spirit, were hitting the clubs with *You Brought The Sunshine* and Vanessa Bell Armstrong caught the full backlash when she signed her secular deal with Jive Records:

"Marvin (Winans) took me into songs without 'Jesus' in them. The company was all for it, they wanted it to cross, and I enjoyed it. No artist should not be able to do what they want to. I had to move on and I believe that these albums reached a secular audience. The gospel world is hard on you though. I heard comments about my make-up and remarks that I was star-crazy, and that all I cared about was money, but that is so far from the truth. I believe I'm doing what God wants me to do - I'm trying to plant a seed."

The Winans themselves were close to the edge on several cuts. *It's Time* was the four Winans brothers plus rapper/producer Teddy Riley on an urban dance tip; BeBe and CeCe Winans went a stage further - *These What Abouts?* was one of many tracks that had no overt gospel identity, while their cover of *I'll Take You There* seemed to acknowledge the Staple Singers as strategic mentors. CeCe Winans hit major cross-over status in spring of '96 with her Whitney Houston duet *Count On Me*, from the *Waiting To Exhale* film soundtrack. This is inspirational modern soul music, conspicuously moral and spiritually uplifting but is it still gospel music? Are such categories irrelevant anyway in the present day? The controversy is rather more serious than the authenticity debates within other music forms. On one side is the argument about style and content, whereby explicit lyrical references to Jesus Christ are obligatory; on the other is the case for drawing in new audiences who might be repelled by what Andrae Crouch calls 'shotgun evangelism.'

Gary Hines, founder of the Sounds of Blackness, the Minneapolis-based choir who have been the only African-American choir to consistently succeed in today's secular marketplace, with massive hits like *I Believe*, *The Pressure*, and *I'm Going All The Way*, has a third and less simplistic perspective:

"The division between the secular and spiritual frames of reference is a false division. It's a European concept that we've taken on but in Africa this division didn't exist, we sang about all areas of life. Even though we're all from the church, the Sounds of Blackness don't describe themselves as a 'gospel' choir per se. We believe that all African-American music is from one source and that for Christians all life is worthy of comment."

Photos: Viv Broughton/A&M Records.

Top: contemporary gospel's most successful artist, CeCe Winans;
below: Minneapolis' hitmakers, the Sounds of Blackness.

The group Commissioned, who launched in 1985 with the album *I'm Going On*, were the template for a completely new style of urban contemporary gospel, as innovative in their way as Andrae Crouch and Rance Allen were in previous decades. Fred Hammond, Karl Reid, Michael Brooks, Michael Williams, Keith Staten and Mitchell Jones, joined later by Marvin Sapp, formed in the same Detroit crucible that fired The Winans. Where Marvin and the guys went one step, Commissioned went two, creating a highly original synthesis of contemporary R&B, urban funk and gospel harmonics. Committed to local church ministries, they were also completely up-front about their purpose:

> "We're giving young people today an alternative to what they're being bombarded with. We're pumpin' but we're singing about Jesus. None of us are looking to sell-out to the world - we have no intention of doing any other kind of music."

The mix didn't appeal to the traditions of gospel and many radio stations boycotted the group in their early years, but Commissioned proved their integrity and won over the sceptics. In March 1990, the Gospel Announcers Guild of the GMWA decided to formally recognise the new music. The category of 'Urban Contemporary Gospel' would serve to describe those musical compositions that *"lyrically express good news about Christ through Proclamation, Revelation and Renewal, yet musically are arranged and produced for compatibility with today's Urban Radio sound."* Though the original group effectively disbanded in 1995, they proved to be a seminal force within modern gospel and far beyond. The Commissioned sound is all over the R&B charts now - million-selling groups like Jodeci and Boyz II Men freely acknowledge Commissioned as the true originals. Is this a film we've seen before?

With both Mattie Moss Clark and James Cleveland now gone from us, who has picked up the choir baton they held out? Perhaps the most significant development in recent years has been the modern choir ensembles of John P. Kee ('the Prince'), Brooklyn's Hezekiah Walker and especially Kirk Franklin and the Family. Dubbed 'new traditional gospel' the phenomenon has achieved astonishing success with a style of music that is two parts old-school to one part urban attitude. Unlike the contemporary sophistication of Anointed, BeBe and CeCe and Commissioned, the new traditionalists are the true heirs of pioneers like Cleveland, Clark and Frank Williams of the Mississippi Mass Choir.

Kee, Walker and Franklin have shown that there is a massive audience for urbanised choir gospel with straight-ahead production values and astute marketing. Working with the independent GospoCentric record label and with no lyrical compromise whatsoever, Kirk Franklin has electrified the whole industry with sales of his eponymous debut album reaching nearly 1.5 million copies in early '96. For a time he was even out-selling secular supergroups like Boyz II Men and TLC. This was unprecedented - no gospel artist had ever achieved these kinds of sales levels before on a debut album.

By the age of just 24, Kirk Franklin had already won two Stellar Awards, two Gospel Music Association Dove Awards, appeared on the Arsenio Hall Show and was drawing crowds of 5000 or more for his concerts. He now moves effortlessly between two distinct personas: at times he's the smartly suited young preacher, Bible in hand, addressing huge congregations with wit and passion; at other times he's the street-wise, urban home-boy hanging with his 17-voice Family, composed of top soloists from the Dallas-Fort Worth area of his Texas home base. In either mode however, there is always a bodyguard on hand.

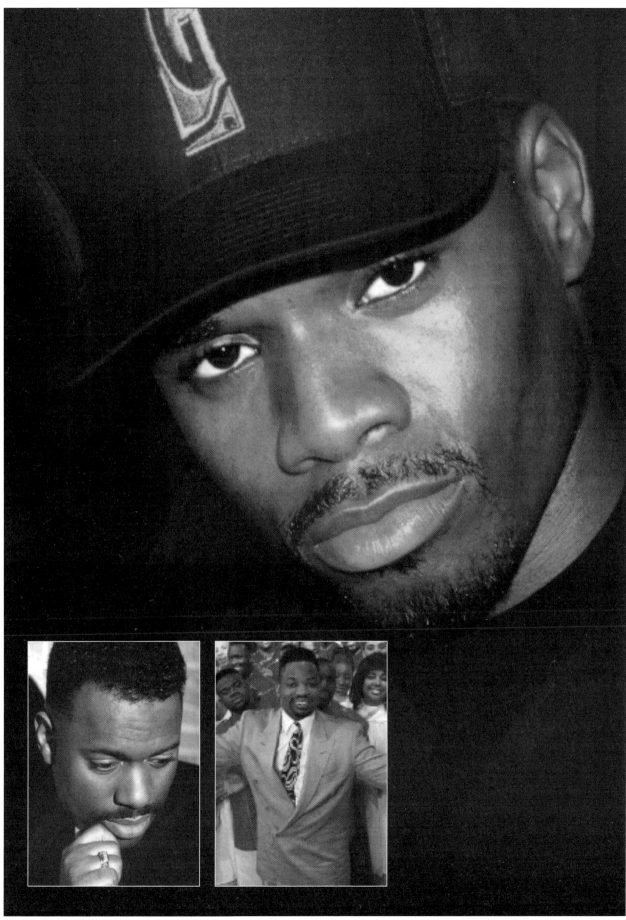

Photos: Viv Broughton/Gospel Today.

The new faces of modern gospel. Main picture: Kirk Franklin;
insets: Rev John P. Kee (L) and Hezekiah Walker.

Born in the tough Riverside neighbourhood, the child of feckless parents who abandoned him, Franklin was raised by his 64 year old great Aunt Gertrude. She collected cans and recycled newspapers to pay for his first piano lessons at four years old. By the age of eleven, he was appointed Minister of Music at Mt. Rose Baptist Church. Adolescence saw the promise squandered - within two years he was running with local gangs:

"I went through a bad time, I drifted away from the church. Like a lot of youngsters in an urban environment, I began doing drugs and drinking with my buddies. Then at 15 one of them was killed - shot to death. It was at that moment I realised, for the first time, it was time for me to stop running away, and that's when I really got back into doing music for the Lord. Today, most of those friends I ran around with are dead or in prison."

Working extensively as writer, arranger and musician with the local DFW Mass Choir and, through Milton Biggham at Savoy, getting the odd writing break with other artists, Kirk Franklin finally put his own choir project together in the summer of '92. *"I borrowed the money from a friend and recorded my songs at Grace Temple in Fort Worth."* Vicki Mack Lataillade, who'd just launched GospoCentric Records with a $6000 loan from her father, remembers the day she first heard those recordings: *"Daryl Coley had this tape in his coat pocket and we were sitting around one day and decided to listen to it. Well I was blown away. I got Kirk on the phone immediately!"* The album, released the following summer, hit No.1 on the Billboard gospel charts and stayed there seemingly for ever, propelling GospoCentric from nowhere to major gospel label status in record time. *"This music has a message,"* Kirk says. *"First and foremost, I'm a preacher. I'm looking for music that convicts people. A lot of the music that makes you 'bump' doesn't necessarily convict you. Sometimes music needs to let you know that you are not your own. I'm a young man and I have the desire to show the world that it's not about the bumping and rocking, to realise that there's forgiveness and salvation at the feet of Jesus. My life's been crazy, but it's been a good crazy,"* he concludes. *"Like the song says, I wouldn't take nothing for my journey now."*

Having acted as the conduit for Kirk Franklin, Daryl Coley now added the role of A&R Manager at GospoCentric to his many and varied duties. Singer, pastor and songwriter, Coley is something of an enigma on the contemporary scene. His vocal technique is legendary - effortless runs, taking in jazz complexity and improvisation (he grew up singing jazz and recently cut a duet with Nancy Wilson) and traditional gospel melismatics. The likes of Luther Vandross rate him as the best male singer bar none.

Oakland, California is his home town - famed as the locale of Walter Hawkins' Love Centre Church and its groundbreaking Choir. The series of four *Love Alive* albums that Walter Hawkins produced in the 70's and 80's dominated gospel for a decade, propelling the young Tramaine Hawkins to national prominence. Keyboardist and vocalist with the Love Centre Choir, Daryl Coley toured extensively with Tramaine, leading to a deal first with the ill-fated Plumbline label, then with Light Records and now with Sparrow. His albums cross many boundaries in gospel and he commands respect from both old and new schools, but he eschews the term 'cross-over':

"When people try to do 'crossover' music it just doesn't work. People don't know where to place you. The interpretation of the music tells where to place you, and that's something that the market decides."

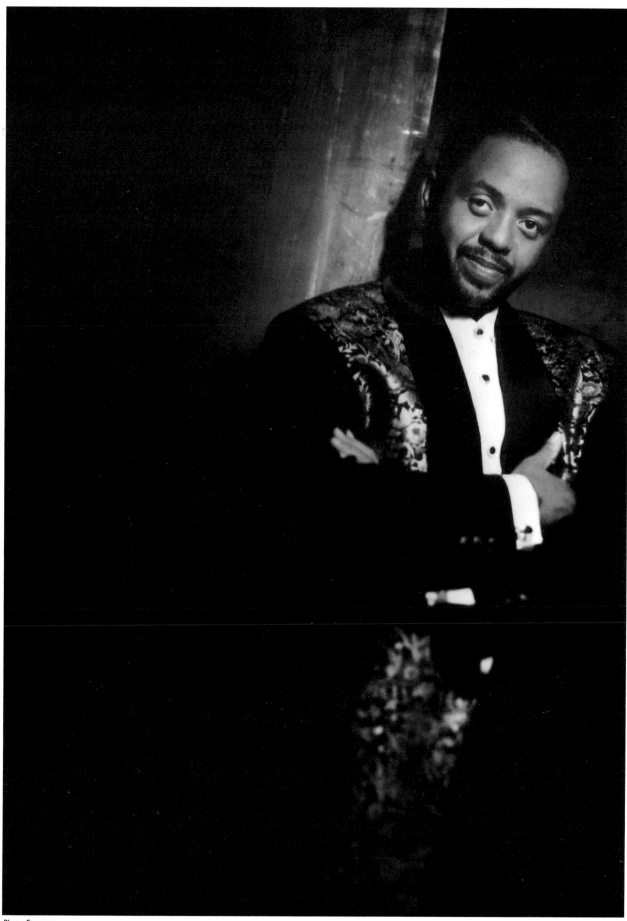

Photo: Sparrow.

Rev Daryl Coley.

At the 1995 Gospel Music Workshop of America, Daryl Coley was called up to sing during the Excellence Awards ceremony. It was unplanned and he was unprepared. He began a 'praise and worship' song, stopped, stilled the band who were picking up behind him and continued acapella. Improvising around Twila Paris' *We Exalt Thee*, Daryl Coley touched every soul in the room, creating a moment of pure epiphany that vividly evoked W. H. Brewster's famous dictum: *a good gospel song is a sermon set to music.*

Yolanda Adams touches people this way too. Like Kirk Franklin, Adams is from Texas, and makes a similarly determined push for a young, urban audience. Originally a Thomas Whitfield protege, this feisty ex-model employs all of Whitfield's complex musical stylings, stirring them with a phenomenal vocal technique that is the equal of Daryl Coley's. In very many ways she is regarded as the new Tramaine Hawkins - both women refer directly to jazz as well as gospel (Stanley Turrentine for Tramaine, Branford Marsalis for Yolanda), both live out their respective marital tragedies on a public platform and, of course, both have model good looks. Whatever else may be expected from gospel in the future, it won't lack for cultural and personal icons.

In this post-Winans era, I've heard some people claim that the male quartet tradition died thirty years ago. That would certainly come as news to The Christianaires, The Williams Brothers, the Canton Spirituals and all the other great vocal groups who are taking that style to another level in the 90s. Put up The Christianaires, for instance, in any gospel context and they will turn the house out as effectively as the Clouds in their time. Originally formed more than fifteen years ago by brothers Paul and Tyrone Porter from Sontag, Mississippi, along with cousins Ronald and Arnold Brown, The Christianaires set gospel alight with a sensational reading of the song *Two Wings* on a James Cleveland tribute album. Six albums and a clutch of industry awards later, they are presently the foremost keepers of the hard quartet flame but they are not alone.

The Jackson Southernaires span two generations of quartet, from the early forties as an amalgam of the Crystal Springs Southernaires and Luther Jennings' family group The World Wonders. The Governor of Mississippi got them a sponsor a year later and for forty three years the Southernaires could be heard every Sunday morning on Jackson radio. *"When we started out, most of the groups were on the same level - we sang a lot of high-style spirituals like Go Down Moses and Wayfaring Stranger,"* recounts Luther. *"We were pulling big crowds into our shows but the money wasn't nothing. I was still working on the meat counter at the grocery on Farish Street. One day in about '65, Dorothy Love Coates pulled me aside in Birmingham and said 'you need to go into the check-up room after concerts.' We didn't have enough knowledge to know we were being taken."*

Thereafter, the Southernaires' earnings improved but it was years before they began to get their due. The soon-to-be main man of gospel in the South, Frank Williams, joined in 1964 and they cut a run of classic albums: *"We did two albums for Peacock, two for ABC, then we signed with Malaco in 1975 where we still record today. Though there were a lot of offers from bigger companies, those folks didn't know how to promote black gospel music."* Every Southernaires album entered the Billboard top ten and four singles have hit the No.1 slot.

Out of the same Mississippi extended family came the Williams Brothers - Melvin, Doug and Henry Green.

Top: Frank Williams and the Mississippi Mass Choir.
Below: The Williams Brothers.

Organised as the 'Little Williams Brothers' by their father in 1960, they've also seen their share of exploitation but emerged unscathed to tell the tale:

> "When we recorded our first album in 1973 with Don Robey on Peacock Records, you know what our payment was? He took us across the street and bought us some hamburgers! No royalties, nothing else...just burgers!"

Seeing that they were selling up to 70,000 albums a time, three of them making No.1, it's not surprising that they finally set up their own company, Blackberry Records, declaring: "It's time for black people in the gospel industry to unite! We're getting peanuts and they're getting rich."

Race in the gospel industry is no less of an explosive issue than in American society generally. As Patrick Henderson of West Angeles COGIC points out, "Eleven o'clock on Sunday morning is still the most segregated hour of the week in America today." The racism endemic to many white churches, and the subsequent divisions within gospel music, are continually experienced by African-Americans but rarely challenged in the public arena.

In 1991, the issue erupted at the predominently white Gospel Music Association (GMA) Convention in Nashville during a series of seminars held to address the business of gospel music. A strong black presence from James Cleveland's GMWA went public with accusations of outright racism, double standards and general downgrading. It provoked a hostile reaction from the white industry execs attending and the story surfaced in Lisa Collins' Billboard column: 'Blacks Pained By Policies of Gospel Association'.

High level talks took place, with both sides airing long-held grievances but little changed in practice, leading Vicki Mack Lataillade to declare recently:

> "There's still a 'good ol' boy' system in the Christian industry. Especially here in Nashville. I believe the walls are breaking down, but you can't really get into the inner circle. But I'm glad we serve a God who doesn't have those barriers. He can make anything happen".

Ownership is fundamental to the problem. Racism is not going to be solved by white people behaving more respectfully (though that would help) but by seeing the ownership of the product and the distribution systems change hands. Racism is always about power and control ... who has it, who exercises it, on whose behalf. The success and growth of black-owned businesses (GospoCentric, Tyscot and Blackberry Records, Bobby Jones TV Productions, Gospel Today magazine and the like) are ultimately far more important than resolutions passed by the GMA. In launching Blackberry Records the same year as the GMA dispute, the Williams Brothers explained the purpose:

> "First of all, this is a vision God gave us. We've been prostituted by some of the major labels, treated fairly by others, but we've always been limited. In the final analysis, you're always limited. We've been in this industry for over 25 years, and it dawned on us that we don't own our own music, our own masters or our own publishing. We write, sing, produce and promote our records - so we felt we should get distribution and go for it!"

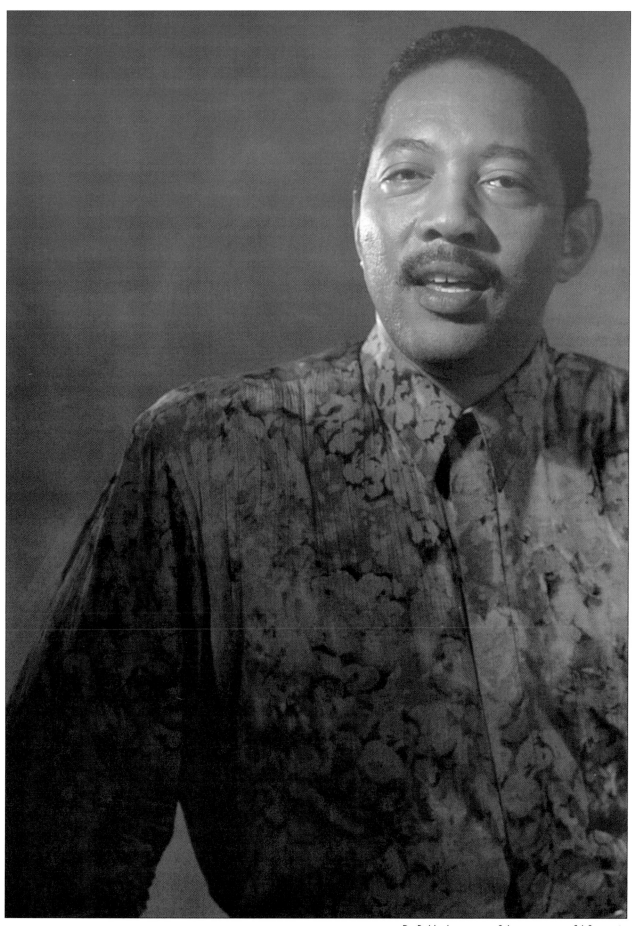

*Dr Bobby Jones; one of the most powerful figures in
gospel music through his networked television shows.*

Top: Commissioned - the urban contemporary template.
Below: acapella masters Alliance, soon to become Take Six.

Photos: Author's collection/
Viv Broughton.

It's 4am in Los Angeles. Quartet Night at the 1995 Gospel Music Workshop of America. The audience, who include Inez Andrews and Joe Ligon, are tired but respectful, waiting for the young lions of new quartet The Christianaires. Up they step, six sharp suits and a band of young players who Willie Mitchell would've killed for, dropping immediately into a deadly serious routine of hard gospel antiphony, reborn southern flavours and evangelistic zeal. The crowd are moved, they're up, they're falling out. Joe Ligon is finally cajoled on stage and the years roll away as he trades with the group like it was '69 all over again.

Quartet is clearly not dead, it's just been re-invented. And how. It's not just the traditional guys who've been taking that squared thing apart and putting it back together again in new ways. The Winans used to deny their quartet heritage but they're clearly in a continuum, as different (and similar) as the Soul Stirrers were different (and similar) to the men who went before them. Take Six, the acapella male group out of the Seventh Day Adventist church, have taken the original complexities of quartet and completely re-worked them with fearsomely advanced vocal harmonies and rhythmic devices redolent of the Golden Gates in their prime. They began at Huntsville College, Alabama as the Gentlemen's Estate Quartet, became the Sounds of Distinction, then Alliance, finally changing their name to Take Six on signing to the mighty Warner Brothers label. Projected modest sales of 25,000 copies of their debut caught Warners on the hop when the album went gold (certified 500,000 units) propelling the sextet into the mainstream big league.

And who's to say that Commissioned or even the group Anointed are not also heirs to the tradition? Although Anointed are a mixed vocal group, quartet was never exclusively male - the Songbirds of the South in the 50s were a particularly fine female quartet, the Angelic Gospel Singers regularly partnered up with the Dixie Hummingbirds and the Lumzy Sisters are currently plowing a similar furrow. The gospel heritage industry - record collectors and historians mostly - should realise that this is living, breathing, dynamic music and it exists to do exactly the same thing today as it always did. Only it won't take quite the same form and nor should it.

Anointed - Steve and Da'dra Crawford, Nee-C Walls and Mary Tiller from Columbus, Ohio are as thrilling in their own way as, say, the Gospel Harmonettes were in theirs, especially at similar points in their respective careers. Unusual in that they feature three women and one man (and he a tenor rather than bass) Anointed nevertheless took the basic principles of quartet gospel singing learned from family group The Crawford Singers, and fashioned them into a contemporary form. When Vicki Winans bumped into them backstage she demanded an impromptu performance in her dressing room: *"I've heard about you. Sing!"* The group demurred. *"We were in awe of her and caught off-guard, so we declined, but she insisted. She said 'you can't be shy in this business' so we did it."* Vicki invited them up to Detroit the following week and they went on to cut one of the most exciting records of the 90s, *Spiritual Love Affair*, winning the Stellar Award for Best New Artist in '95 and three Dove Awards in '96. Now a trio following Mary Tiller's departure, Anointed are still the main contemporary act to watch out for.

Gospel today extends its varied traditions. Out to one side are those like the Sounds of Blackness, re-casting the mould of 'message music', as the Staple Singers did in the 70s. That is, danceable music with lyrical integrity and cross-over potential but only barely within gospel's broad church.

Yolanda Adams.

Photo: Tribute.

Solidly in the middle stand the current community and mass choirs, the firm foundations - Mississippi, Chicago, Georgia, LA, New Jersey, the Thompson Community Singers, Brooklyn Tabernacle, Douglas Miller, the many COGIC State and National choirs and the younger chorales of O'Landa Draper, Rickey Grundy and Ricky Dillard. The modern choir sound is more disciplined, more tightly arranged but still an exhilarating experience for singers and audience alike.

Anointed and Kirk Franklin exemplify gospel's current front line, but the inspired tradition also continues through the committed music of the Kurt Carr Singers, Angela Spivey, Rev James Moore and the immensely gifted Richard Smallwood Singers. As the studio production of gospel finally comes of age through people like Keith Thomas, Bubba Smith and the late maestro Thomas Whitfield, the vocal priorities of the music once again come to the fore. Not since the 1960s, when gospel began to collapse under the weight of cheap R&B, has the human voice and its uniquely personal expression of faith been accorded such a pre-eminent position in the recorded mix. The best of the new gospel records are superbly crafted and produced, bringing all the artistry of modern studio techniques to bear on the central vocal witness.

Where in the recent past, engineers and producers (such as they were) would take a gospel group and attempt to reduce spiritual fire to an unholy mess of third-rate pop, now there is evidence of gospel creating its own professional standards. There is a fresh recognition that everything matters - that for a singer to be heard and a message delivered, a proper context must be created. It's a simple lesson but a long time in the learning, that a great performance can be destroyed utterly by the circumstances of recording and presentation. Through radio and television, gospel music has made enormous strides. Since 1975 Dr Bobby Jones, through his networked shows on Black Entertainment Television, has brought gospel directly into 33 million homes and in so doing has created a world constituency for the music.

Gospel in the 90s still works best as the Word of God delivered in the most fundamental way: as one heart speaking to another, as one soul to another. Everything else is just an adjunct to this, subverting or enhancing the process. It's not about style - whatever the genre, musicians can underpin or they can overbear, arrangers can channel a song to greater effect or they can deflect its impact, producers can elevate the witness or they can drown it in superfluity.

Secular music invariably represents what people already are. Gospel music, in stark contrast, must represent the highest they can ever become. Take Anointed or Daryl Coley's albums, as proof that it can be done. This is modern gospel that succeeds on all levels: spiritually, artistically, technically and, yes, commercially. For there is a hunger to hear gospel music that *confronts*, rather than reflects, popular culture.

Yet, however advanced the music becomes, gospel tradition is never far away. Perhaps it's all part of the same hunger, but one of the biggest gospel successes of the 80s was the down-home country gospel of a North Carolina couple, Rev F. C. Barnes and Rev Janice Brown. Their album *Rough Side of The Mountain* sat at No. 1 in the gospel charts for months, proving that there'll always be plenty of room for unsophisticated saints singing unsophisticated songs.

The Fairfield Four, an astonishing seventy five years on from their origins at Fairfield Baptist Church in Nashville, are currently achieving the greatest recording and concert successes of their career, while still singing exactly the way they did then. (Even the **Golden Gate Quartet** are still going strong - I came across them in a tiny village in the **South of France** not so long ago, playing in a packed out bull-ring to a highly appreciative audience.)

For as much as it challenges, gospel still serves to comfort and strengthen when the burden gets too heavy. As **Inez Andrews**, now in her seventies, observes:

> *"If you've never had an urge to read the Bible, maybe a song will inspire you to. Everybody don't go to church and some people don't want to be saved. But when trouble comes, they want to have something they can reach out to. And most times, if it's not the Bible, it's a song."*

And **Inez'** compatriot from the **Caravans**, **Shirley Caesar**, has few doubts about what works best for her:

> *"My records had gone in the contemporary direction during the 1980s. But my mother, on her death bed, made me promise that I would return to that old time Gospel feeling, the more traditional material, that spiritual fervour that people expect of me. Some people thought that I would attract a wider audience if I sang Contemporary Christian Music with an orchestra, but I found that it didn't really appeal to them and it didn't please my long-time friends. I've found that mama was right, that good old Gospel music that tells the story is what people want."*

Marvin Winans, pastor now of his **Perfecting Church** in Detroit, has taken some criticism in his time, but his experience has been salutory. For him, gospel music is ultimately not about form but about substance:

> *"The anointing of God will only rest upon the Word of God. Where there is no Word, there can be no anointing. So it is important that our songs are scripturally correct, because that is the only way the anointing can rest. And if you do not have the anointing of God, then you just sing. That's all."*

And **Marvin's** generation can take encouragement from the words of a **Chicago** veteran of the Dorsey era. Speaking at the venerable age of 70 and at a time when **The Winans** were all over the gospel charts, **Kenneth Morris** observed:

> *"It does for the contemporaneous people of today exactly what our music did for the contemporaneous people in the 1940s, 1950s and 1960s. Music evolves exactly like everything else. These are facts. So, they were upset when I came along. A lot of people said I was playing the devil's music. They didn't want to hear it in the church. Well, our generation is saying the same thing of the young people today. That it's nothing but the world's music. We are telling the children of today exactly the same thing our parents told us. And in the same words. So it is no difference. Some of these songs, I can't even play them. I confess the difficulty. The children don't have any difficulty. They don't stop because they are being criticised. They are enjoying what they are doing. People are still being saved and coming to Christ. So who are we to argue? The music goes on."*

It sure does. ❖

Photo: Colin Patterson.

Steve and Da'dra Crawford and
Nee-C Walls - Anointed.

INDEX

INDEX

Photos: Author's collection/Horst Lippman.